# MCCLEAVER

IF ONE DOMINO FALLS, THEY ALL FALL

CLIFTON WELSH

This is a work of fiction. Names, characters, places, and incidents either are the product of the author's imagination or are used fictitiously. Any resemblance to actual persons, living or dead, events, or locales is entirely coincidental.

All rights reserved. No part of this book may be reproduced or used in any manner without written permission of the copyright owner except for the use of quotations in a book review.

First paperback edition April 2022
Contact the author at: CliftonWelsh33@gmail.com

Book design: Jack McNeil

Copyright © 2022 by Clifton Welsh

ISBN: 978-1-7334601-5-6

# TABLE OF CONTENTS

1. Uninvited Guest ....................................................... 5
2. The Offer ................................................................ 9
3. Session One: The Perfect Cereal ........................... 18
4. Session Two: A Different Absolute ....................... 29
5. Session Three: Absolute Truth-Giver .................... 37
6. Session Four: Postmodern Domino ...................... 52
7. Session Five: Biblical Domino ............................... 66
8. Session Six: Thirteen Books .................................. 72
9. Session Seven: Two Redactors .............................. 81
10. Session Eight: Domino of the Flood ................... 90
11. Session Nine: Time Defined .............................. 100
12. Session Ten: Piece of the Puzzle ........................ 111
13. Session Eleven: Event Theory ............................ 130
14. Session Twelve: Running the Race ..................... 137
15. Session Thirteen: On Haloes .............................. 150
16. Session Fourteen: Two Equivalent Timelines ..... 157
17. Session Fifteen: The Beginning ......................... 168
18. Session Sixteen: The Ending ............................. 178
19. Session Seventeen: Importance of Equivalence ... 187
20. Session Eighteen: A Common Event ................. 201
21. Session Nineteen: A New Evolution .................. 214
22. Session Twenty: Origin of Dinosaurs ................. 224
23. Session Twenty-One: The Babel Question ......... 231
24. Session Twenty-Two: Final Question ................ 245
25. Session Twenty-Three: Final Answer ................. 265
26. Final Exam ......................................................... 278
    Questions for Reflection and Discussion ............ 281
    Acknowledgements .............................................. 304

CHAPTER 1

# UNIVITED GUEST

"We live in a world in which there are no absolutes," begins the professor in my philosophy class. "That means you are free to..." He stops in mid-sentence and stiffens as he stares toward the back of the lecture hall. Then, with a hesitation in his voice, he speaks. "Professor."

"Erik," returns an old man's voice.

The oddity of the exchange captures me. Today's lecture is being given by Erik Wadford, Ph.D., Associate Professor of Philosophy. Professor Wadford addressed the old man as "Professor" but, in his reply, the old man addressed Professor Wadford by his first name, Erik. The implication is that the old man holds a higher academic station than does Professor Wadford.

Professor Wadford regains his composure and continues his lecture. "You are free to choose your own values. That is because there is no such thing as 'truth' in the sense of some overarching principle to which everyone is obliged to agree and therefore to which everyone is obliged to conform. There exist no external constraints limiting your personal freedom. There are no absolutes governing your choices of values and moral. . ."

My mind drifts from the lecture toward the old man making his way down the aisle to my right. I sit in the center section about two-thirds of the way back from the front of the lecture hall. The old man finds an empty aisle seat on my row directly across from my section. He steadies himself with his cane as he takes his seat.

The lecture fights it way back into my mind, "...have many choices. Make choices that advance principles of equality and nondiscrimination. Do what you can to advance the quality of life for everyone in your community. Devote your energies to abolishing prejudice, racism, intolerance..."

The old man is dressed in a rumpled brown suit jacket with matching pants. His shirt is a deep purple turtleneck. His pure white hair is tussled in waves that break downward nearly covering his ears. He leans back in his seat with his arms folded across his chest.

"...advance social justice and economic equality." Professor Wadford pauses while looking over his class and finishes. "Any questions?"

After a few moments an elderly voice breaks the silence. "I have a question."

Professor Wadford nods toward the old man. All eyes in the classroom turn toward him.

The elderly voice rises in volume. "You began your lecture with the presupposition that there are no absolutes. My question is this: Is your claim speculative or definitive?"

Professor Wadford stares at the old man, giving him time to explain what he means by his question.

The old man continues. "If your claim that there are no absolutes is speculative, then you are saying that there are no absolutes, but you are not sure. In this case you have to allow for the possibility of the existence of one or more absolutes, however unlikely that prospect may be. On the other hand, if your claim is definitive, then you are certain that there are no absolutes. In that event, your presupposition becomes a self-contradiction. You say there are no absolutes, but you have made one. The statement, 'There are no absolutes' becomes an absolute."

Professor Wadford stares at the old man for a moment longer then turns toward the class. "If there are no further questions, then class is dismissed."

CHAPTER 2

# THE OFFER

Instantly the room is filled with sounds of shuffling feet and overlapping voices. The clamor diminishes as students depart the lecture hall. I remain seated. So does the old man. Finally, there are only three people left in the room - Professor Wadford, the old man, and me.

Professor Wadford departs the lecture platform and walks up the aisle toward the old man. The old man stands and there is a brief exchange in voices too soft for me to hear as Professor Wadford passes by. Then the old man turns to leave the room. I follow.

I catch up with him in the corridor outside of lecture hall. "Excuse me, sir. May I walk with you?"

The old man stops, turns, and smiles. "Of course, you may walk with me."

We stride out of the classroom building onto the campus square. "Do you know Professor Wadford?"

"Certainly. I was Chair of the Biology Department when Professor Wadford was brought on at the University."

"Wow! So, you're, ah, er…"

"Professor Stuart McCleaver, although I now have the title, 'Emeritus' since I retired two years ago. And you are?"

"Wellington. Connor Wellington. I'm a senior majoring in biology. I am minoring in journalism. I am also taking courses in religion and philosophy."

"What kind of biology?"

"General biology. But I'm now interested in evolution science. Problem is, some of the material doesn't make sense to me. Seems contradictory."

"I am familiar with evolution science. Now that I am getting on in years I, on occasion, have bad days. On some of my bad days, really bad days, when I awake, I find myself questioning whether there is any such thing as 'evolution science.' But then, when I come to my senses, I realize that evolution science is really similar to forensic science except that the obvious has been ruled out *a priori*."

Astonished at his answer, I push back. "What? Are you saying that you don't accept evolution? If science has proven anything, science has proven evolution!"

"Didn't you hear Professor Wadford tell us that there are no absolutes? No absolutes, no truth, just truth claims. If postmodern theory is correct, evolution is just another truth claim."

"But there is a mountain of scientific evidence that supports evolution!"

"Most proponents of truth claims are able to assemble facts to support their claims."

Not knowing what to do or what to say, I walk along with Professor McCleaver for a few minutes. Then he stops and looks directly at me. "You seem to be a student who is seriously searching for answers regarding these matters. I can assure you that you won't get the answers you seek by walking across campus with me. Perhaps you would like to meet with me to pursue these topics more deeply."

Surprised by his invitation, I reply impulsively,

"Yes, I would."

"Very well. What is your schedule for tomorrow?"

"I have a class in the morning but I am free in the afternoon."

"Then meet me at the grocery entrance to Walmart tomorrow afternoon at two."

With that the old professor turns and crosses a street toward a residential neighborhood next to campus. I continue toward Wally's Pub to meet some friends.

Sean Dickerson and Megan Butterfield are already there and have secured a table for four. Sean is also majoring in biology and is planning to go on to graduate school to study microbiology. His long black hair is swept to the back of his head and tied in a clipped-off pony tail. He wears dark-rimmed glasses but by no means is he a geek. Sean is not given to excessive conversation. He is a quiet listener, but when he does say something, it is worth the time to listen.

Megan is one of Sean's friends. She is planning a career in teaching at the secondary school level. Somewhat thin, Megan is attractive, but not beautiful. Nevertheless, we guys often joke that Megan is the only reason our table gets served.

Sometimes she is bright, bubbly, conversational, and funny. At other times she is quiet, even moody. Once she confided that she was distressed by family problems.

I step to the table and rest my pack of books on the floor by an empty chair. Sitting down, I glance at both Sean and Megan. They nod. I start the conversation. "Great choice for a table. Right next to the window. We can watch the pretty girls walk by."

"There is only one pretty girl you need to watch," retorts Megan without looking up.

"Out there they are pretty; in here they are dangerous," smiles Sean.

"Be on your guard," warns Megan.

A waiter approaches and stands next to my chair. "What can I get you?"

"A beer."

"Any kind?"

"Whatever they're having; whatever you have on tap."

While I wait for my beverage, I query, "Any sign of Jason? There is only one empty chair. The later he comes, the more likely one chair will not be enough."

Megan smiles. "Jason really is social."

Sean looks up. "Chances are less then fifty-fifty that he shows up alone."

Jason Kend is a business major. He hails from a wealthy family in a Chicago suburb, Oak Park I believe. His father runs a large insurance business and is a representative in the Illinois state legislature. Gregarious and friendly, Jason follows in his father's footsteps. His well-styled sandy-brown hair crowns a thin face that accentuates his broad smile. Jason loves good conversation but becomes impatient with small-talk, especially when the small-talk is off subject.

My beer arrives. In silence we three slowly dissolve into our individual worlds. Suddenly Sean looks up. "I see Jason and he is not alone. Looks like we need another chair."

Sean jumps up, borrows an empty chair from a nearby table, and pushes it over to join us. Then he and Megan slide their chairs toward me to give our arrivals more leg room.

Jason enters Wally's Pub with a broad smile and immediately approaches our table with his friend in tow. The strange scene captures me. Following Jason is a man who is larger than he is in every respect. A bushy head of pitch-black hair rises above a block-shaped face. It looks somewhat like Jason is leading an All-American lineman of the college football team. "Hi everyone. This is Demetrius Broadinski."

Sean and I stand and shake hands with our new visitor. Megan smiles and says, "Hello."

Jason continues, "Demetrius and I attend sociology class together. He asked a question the instructor couldn't answer. After class we started talking about it while standing in the Quad so, since it was getting late, I suggested that Demetrius join us here."

First impressions are not always accurate. At Sean's prompting Demetrius readily tells us about himself. He is attending the University on a full four-year scholarship. A senior majoring in mathematics and theoretical physics, he has already completed the core coursework needed for graduation, so is taking classes in other fields of study such as sociology. That is how he came to meet Jason.

When he finishes, I ponder that, if the table were a boat and brilliance had weight, then the table would be tipped toward Demetrius. I suspect the others feel the same way as we consume our meals in silence.

After a while I look up as I sip from my glass of beer and notice that Demetrius is giving me a hard look. "Connor, did I see you walking along the Quad with an old man this afternoon?"

"You mean Professor Stuart McCleaver?"

"McCleaver!" exclaims Sean. "You were with Professor McCleaver? He was my instructor in general biology three years ago."

"Actually, Professor Stuart McCleaver, Emeritus. He retired two years ago."

"That explains why I haven't seen him since then. He was the best instructor I've had for any course at this university. He could explain the most complex subjects through simple analogies."

"Hmmm," I ponder. "I may soon be exposed to McCleaver's analogies."

"How so?" queries Jason.

"Professor McCleaver showed up in my philosophy class today and questioned my instructor's lecture."

"Who is your instructor?" interrupts Megan.

"Professor Erik Wadford. Anyway, McCleaver

challenged Wadford's fundamental presupposition that there are no absolutes."

I notice that the eyes of all four of my table partners are fixed on me. "I caught up with him after class and we talked as we walked across campus."

"So how does that expose you to McCleaver's analogies?" asks Sean.

"McCleaver offered to meet me for further discussions. At the entrance to Walmart."

"Maybe he wants you to help him select a new wardrobe," laughs Demetrius.

Jason concurs. "A purple turtleneck in a brown suit? Maybe Demetrius is on to something. The man does need help."

CHAPTER 3

# SESSION ONE: THE PERFECT CEREAL

Two thoughts occupy my mind the next day as I depart campus for the local Walmart store. *First, it's common to see a student with green hair, or a badly colored tee-shirt on the front of which is emblazoned some crude slogan, or a pair of tattered jeans, or worse. But a professor in a brown suit with a purple turtleneck shirt? Somehow a professor so bedecked defies convention. Really, what is the reason for the 'Emeritus' stamped at the end of McCleaver's pedigree? Second, if the master teacher educates by analogies, what does Walmart have to offer that enlightens fundamental presuppositions of postmodern philosophy?*

I arrive at the grocery entrance to the Walmart

store shortly before two in the afternoon. Professor McCleaver is already there.

"Good afternoon, Connor."

"Professor."

"Follow me."

I follow the professor into the store. He leads me through the grocery section and stops at the cereal aisle. As he guides me past box after box of cereals arrayed four shelves high, he says, "I want you to take note of the vast number of cereal offerings. I want you to find the perfect cereal. I will be at the Student Union faculty lounge at this time tomorrow. Meet me there and we will discuss your findings."

Professor McCleaver turns and walks away.

I stand in front of the wall of cereals and ponder. *He wants me to find the perfect cereal? Hmmm. Is there any such thing as a perfect cereal? How would one define a perfect cereal?*

At 2:00 PM Friday I enter the Student Union and head toward the faculty lounge. Professor McCleaver sits alone in a corner booth enjoying his coffee. He sees me coming. "Welcome, Connor. I trust you had an informative afternoon yesterday. Did you find the perfect cereal?"

"Nope."

"Why not?"

"After you left, I did some thinking. First, I had no criteria by which to define what constitutes a 'perfect' cereal. Second, I had no idea whether there exists a 'perfect' cereal."

"What did you do then?"

"I watched one-hundred and sixty-three people select cereal. I tabulated the number of selections for each brand and constructed a list ordered from the most selected cereals to the least."

"What did you discover?"

"A lot of cereals were not selected. The brand most selected was Kellogg's Corn Flakes."

"Out of the one-hundred and sixty-three people you sampled, how many selected Corn Flakes?"

"Twenty-nine."

"Twenty-nine? Does that mean Kellogg's Corn Flakes is the perfect cereal?"

"I don't think so."

"Why not?"

"Simply because Corn Flakes was the most selected

doesn't make it the perfect cereal, does it?"

Professor McCleaver lifts his coffee mug, takes a sip, pauses for a moment and then places the mug back on the table. All the while he studies me. Finally, he speaks. "Connor, it was for the purpose of education that I took you to the Walmart cereal aisle. I could have given you a dozen books, all authored by authorities in the field of postmodern theory, all expertly written, ideas clearly explained, and, as regards deep thought, all authors nearly brain-dead."

He takes a deep breath and continues. "No absolutes? No 'truth'? Just truth 'claims?' My God! What an imbeciles' playground postmodernism is! Connor, every person has a truth claim does he not?"

"I guess so."

"Now suppose I announce that my truth claim is truer than your truth claim."

"That depends on how true your truth claim is."

"You are getting the idea. But facts have nothing to do with it. My truth claim wins because of popular opinion. It's not facts that matter. Facts were the modernist approach. Today, it's polls that matter. It's a new form of mob rule. Think of it, Connor. If I can assemble enough supporters, especially supporters with hands on levers of power, my truth claim can be made *the* truth. Actually, my truth claim can be made absolute simply by a mob overthrow of less popular truth claims."

Professor McCleaver sips some coffee and continues. "Have you heard of 'cancel culture' – the practice of removing people with unpopular truth claims from social media?"

"Yes. Someone makes an idiotic claim about someone or something, and a lot of people who know better challenge him."

"What is the basis for determining a claim to be idiotic or for deciding who knows better?"

"Hmmm. I don't know."

"Allow me to give you an example of mob overthrow of an unpopular truth claim. Early on during the 2020 global sickness, a claim was made that the virus escaped from a research facility. Do you recall the reaction of those who think of themselves as gatekeepers of truth claims?"

"Those who made those claims were cast as 'conspiracy nuts' whose lies were undermining the truth. Messages by those people were blocked and/or accounts suspended by the providers."

"What was the basis for the judgments by the gatekeepers against those who promoted the escape truth claim?"

"Er, I don't know."

"They uncritically accepted a narrative put forth by what they saw as the 'enlightened opinion' at the time – truth claims by other elites whose opinions they valued. Then they pulled their levers of power to make their truth claim *the* truth by silencing a less popular truth claim even though the escape claim has a basis in fact."

McCleaver gulps some coffee and continues. "So, Connor, what is the modus operandi of the cancel culture?"

"Ignorance?"

"Add in ideology, political or fiduciary gain, hidden agendas, bigotry, prejudice, and elitism. All one has to do is to assemble enough supporters with hands on levers of power to make his truth claim *the* truth."

I stare at the old professor as he continues.

"Since the underlying premise of postmodernism

is not fact-based but opinion-based, there is no way of 'knowing' whether one truth claim is better than any others. What makes a truth claim 'more true' with respect to other truth claims depends on how many people can be persuaded to believe it!"

Professor McCleaver's eyes flash with intensity. "Connor, each brand of cereal on Walmart's cereal aisle is analogous to a truth claim. How 'true' each truth claim is depends on how many people buy it."

I ask, "So then, since twenty-nine people selected Kellogg's Corn Flakes, does that mean Corn Flakes is more 'true' than other cereals?"

"It does. But only in popularity. Postmodernism gives us no means to define what is really true because there are no absolutes with which to create standards of truth. And that brings me to the perfect cereal. Why didn't you find the perfect cereal?"

"Well, thanks to you, I now understand why my approach could not lead me to the perfect cereal. But still, I have no means to identify the perfect cereal, so I have no way of knowing whether a perfect cereal exists."

"Then, what are your conclusions?"

"The perfect cereal was on the shelf, but I lacked the means to find it."

"Or?"

"The perfect cereal doesn't exist?"

"So, the perfect cereal exists, but you lack the knowledge needed to find it, or I am lying and really there is no such thing as a perfect cereal."

"Yes. I guess so."

"I would like to offer a third explanation. The perfect cereal was removed from the shelf before we arrived at Walmart."

"Why would someone do that?"

"That is the subject for our next session. Coffee here, Tuesday, at two?"

Since I am already at the Student Union, I drift into one of the study rooms and read through one of my assignments. At around five-thirty I depart to the cafeteria for dinner. After having purchased my selections, I search for a table. Jason Kend and Demetrius Broadinski are dining nearby so I approach them. "Hi, guys. May I join you?"

"No objections," smiles Jason.

I take my seat and begin devouring my selections.

Jason interrupts my progress. "Let's see, Connor. Yesterday was the day you were going to Walmart to help Professor McCleaver buy some clothes."

Laughter.

Speaking deliberately, I reply. "That would have been easy."

"What did he do?"

"Remember when Sean told us that Professor McCleaver teaches by analogies? Well, he does. He took me to the cereal aisle and assigned me to find the perfect cereal and report back to him this afternoon."

"I'm interested in knowing what is the perfect cereal," laughs Jason. "But, not really."

Facing Jason, I reply. "You should be. I will never look at cereal the same way again."

"What did McCleaver say?" inquires Demetrius.

"I took a count of which cereals customers were selecting and found that Kellogg's Corn Flakes is the most popular brand. McCleaver tied the number of cereals to truth claims, and then said that some truth claims are truer than other truth claims because more people believe them."

"I see no basis for that," interrupts Jason.

"McCleaver claims that the more people who can be persuaded to believe a truth claim, the truer the truth claim becomes. Finally, those with opposing or unpopular truth claims are silenced."

"I don't see that happening," replies Jason, "... although I can think of some opinions that *should* be silenced."

"It does happen," I counter. "Remember the student group that held a meeting last fall, and a group of protesters showed up and shouted down the speaker?"

"That was an exercise of freedom of expression."

"It was also denying a viewpoint from being heard. Do you remember two years ago, when the commencement committee selected a speaker, and a group of about twenty professors wrote asking the administration to disinvite that speaker because his views were not consistent with current thought?"

"That was an exercise of freedom of expression."

"McCleaver takes it further. He sees what you call 'freedom of expression' as morphing into 'denial of expression' and into 'cancel culture,' where gatekeepers of social media get someone 'canceled' or ostracized or removed because their views don't fit with currently promoted truth claims."

Demetrius looks on pensively. "I am beginning to smell the stench of tyranny. My ancestors grew up in Eastern Europe under Russian socialism. My grandfather told me that Josef Stalin had lots of photographs taken to highlight the glories of communism. When someone fell out favor, Stalin had that person purged from his photographs. In a way, these people were 'canceled.' Later, when someone disagreed with prevailing communist thought, he was simply removed to the gulags. He disappeared; he was 'canceled'."

"Hmmm," muses Jason. "I hadn't seen it that way before. If McCleaver is correct, then postmodernism doesn't lead to personal freedom as we have been taught. It leads to tyranny dressed up in a different suit of clothes."

He turns to me. "Connor, are you going to meet with the professor again?"

"Yes, on Tuesday."

"Well, we meet at Wally's Pub on Wednesday. I will be looking forward to hearing what you find out."

CHAPTER 4

# SESSION TWO: A DIFFERENT ABSOLUTE

At two o'clock on Tuesday Professor McCleaver is sitting at his favorite booth with his coffee mug on the table in front of him. After the mind-stretching session of last week I am uneasy as to what to expect. I sit down and address him pensively.

"Professor."

"Connor," he replies with a smile. "Do you remember where we left off last week?"

"We were discussing the perfect cereal. You summarized the possibilities."

"Which were?"

"First, the perfect cereal does not exist. Second,

the perfect cereal exists but we don't have the means to identify it. Third, the perfect cereal exists, but had been removed from the shelf before we arrived at Walmart."

Professor McCleaver looks at me with a puzzled expression for a moment. "Oh, yes. Yes! That's where we were. Now I remember. The perfect cereal!"

He takes a sip of coffee. "In our cereal analogy, the perfect cereal represents the absolute. Absolute truth if you prefer. One can argue that absolute truth doesn't exist. Another can argue that absolute truth may exist, but we don't have the wherewithal to know what it is. Or a third argument can be made that absolute truth does exist, but has been removed from the shelf *a priori*."

Professor McCleaver lifts his mug to his lips. Looking over the top of the mug he queries. "Connor, do you remember Professor Wadford's opening statement, his presupposition?"

"We live in a world in which there are no absolutes."

"Which of our conclusions do you think he had in mind?"

"The first two conclusions. Either there are

no absolutes or, if there are, we cannot know what they are."

"Suppose he had all three conclusions in mind. Do you remember my question to him at the end of his lecture?"

"You asked if his presupposition was speculative or definitive."

"And his answer?"

"He didn't answer."

"Why do you think he didn't answer?"

"I don't know."

"Professor Wadford is no intellectual lightweight. He knows how to manipulate naiveté. I have no doubt that he understands all three of our conclusions. He also knows that his presupposition is valid only for the first two conclusions. If he had answered 'speculative,' he would have admitted to the possibility of an absolute. If he had answered 'definitive,' he would have created his own absolute. In either case, by not answering my question, he avoided turning attention to absolutes and left it to the class to believe that there are none."

"Frankly, I am puzzled by the third conclusion.

What does it really mean?"

"*A priori* removal of the absolute?"

"Yes."

"Several meanings. First, suppose there exists a perfect cereal. Suppose the perfect cereal was placed on the shelf along with all the other cereals. What do you think would happen?"

"Customers would eventually discover the perfect cereal and stop buying all the others."

"Yes. Eventually, all the other cereals would be discontinued. As regards truth claims, the presence of an absolute truth would eliminate the need to invent personal truth claims and, more importantly, there would be no need for teachers of postmodern theory who tell us that we should."

Professor McCleaver sips from his coffee mug. "Second, do you remember my assertions about competing truth claims, that I could argue that my truth claim is truer than your truth claim?"

"Yes. You said that the way you could make your truth claim truer than my truth claim is to get more people to agree with you than would agree with me."

"And, if I could persuade those whose hands are on

the levels of power, I could raise my truth claim to the level of an absolute truth claim."

"You said that you would also work to suppress all other truth claims."

"Yes, but it wouldn't have to be me. Any elite with his hands on the levers of power could impose his truth claim on the masses."

The old professor sips more coffee as he continues. "Professor Wadford led the class to believe that all truth claims are valid did he not?"

"Yes."

"You have your truth claim and I have my truth claim and we all respect each other's truth claim?"

"Yes."

"However, didn't Professor Wadford lay out criteria by which you were to formulate your truth claims?"

"Yes. Professor Wadford told us that postmodern theory is the way to pure democracy, inclusion, and tolerance…"

Professor McCleaver smiles as I complete the sentence. "…and, holding to an absolute truth, which is the same as claiming possession of a superior truth claim, which all must recognize as true, is the way into judgmentalism, intolerance, tyranny, and racism?"

"Then it seems from Professor Wadford's perspective, that possession of an absolute truth is not to be desired. When he opened his lecture with the presupposition that 'we live in a world in which there are no absolutes,' he removed the perfect cereal from the cereal shelves *a priori*, did he not?"

"I see! banning an absolute doesn't eliminate the absolute. All banning the absolute does is open the way for elites to put forth their truth claim as a false absolute."

"And what if Professor Wadford is one of the elites?"

"He would be manipulating us to abandon an absolute in order to accept an opinion as a substitute absolute."

"For the elites, postmodern theory is a means to power. For the rest of us, postmodern theory is a fool's errand."

"All this seems so political."

"Political correctness is the term," continues the old professor. "The elites have a truth claim of their own manufacture and they are using what means they have to force... Oh, I shouldn't use the word 'force'... Let's say the elites 'encourage' us to acquiesce to their truth claim as an absolute in the name of peace and tolerance."

"I get it! Professor Wadford tells us there are no absolutes and we are free to frame our own truth claims. Then he directs how we should frame our truth claims with words and phrases such as principles of equality, nondiscrimination, eradication of prejudice and racism, social justice, and economic equality. All the while, the elites holding levers of power are establishing their own truth claims as false absolutes through intimidation via political correctness and cancel culture."

Professor McCleaver lifts his mug for another sip of coffee. "Ugh! Coffee is cold!" Then he stares at me. "I have answered your questions regarding my presence and comments during Professor Wadford's lecture, have I not?"

"Well, yes and no."

"You still have unanswered questions?"

"You have shown me what postmodern theory is, and the motives behind it, but I still have a question regarding 'absolute' truth."

"Which is?"

"What is an absolute truth?"

Professor McCleaver takes a deep breath and exhales, twisting his lips to direct his breath upward causing the waves of white hair on his forehead to flutter. "Okay. Suppose there is an absolute truth. What would we call the person who puts forth an absolute truth?"

"An absolute truth-giver?"

"As you look across the landscape of truth claim givers, who might be a good candidate for an absolute truth-giver?"

I stare at the professor in silence.

"Connor, I think you are broaching a subject that needs more thought. I've had enough for this afternoon. Why not meet again Thursday, same time, same place?"

CHAPTER 5

# SESSION THREE: ABSOLUTE TRUTH-GIVER

On Wednesday evening, I approach Wally's Pub anticipating a time of lively discussion. Sean Dickerson, Jason Kend, and Demetrius Broadinski have secured a table and five chairs. Megan Butterfield arrives a few minutes later with a friend. Sean secures a sixth chair while Megan introduces Salome Kublish. There is a round of mutual introductions and Salome takes her seat as part of our Wednesday discussion group. She is dressed in tight-fitting denim pants and wears a loose-fitting sweatshirt that obscures some of her physical features. The smooth skin on her pretty face is crowned by dark brown hair. Her eyes narrow in a stern expression and she seems not given to smiling.

After our conversation has normalized and our servings of snacks and drinks are placed in front of us, Jason turns our interest to postmodern theory. "Sean, Megan, I think we should bring you up to speed on conversations we had with Connor during dinner last Friday. Recall our gathering last Wednesday when Connor told us that he was going to meet with Professor McCleaver at Walmart on Thursday afternoon."

"Yeah, I remember," offers Sean. "We joked about Connor assisting McCleaver in selecting a new wardrobe."

Laughter.

"Well," continues Jason as his smile evaporates. "Connor met with McCleaver Thursday afternoon and again on Friday. Then he dined with Demetrius and me on Friday evening. So, Connor, why don't you brief the others on what you told us?"

I begin. "Two things. By the way, Sean, Professor McCleaver really is a master of analogies. First thing: Last Wednesday I told you that Professor McCleaver entered Professor Wadford's class and challenged his premise that there are no absolutes. What I didn't tell you is that Professor Wadford didn't answer McCleaver's question. Second thing: Fast forward to Thursday. McCleaver took me to the cereal aisle at Walmart and claimed that the large number of different cereals could be used as an analogy to understand postmodern theory. He told me to find the perfect cereal and report back to him on Friday afternoon."

"There is no such thing as a 'perfect' cereal!" interrupts Megan.

"Agreed!" follows Sean emphatically.

Laughter.

"That was my report," I reply to regain control of the conversation. "When I met McCleaver Friday afternoon, I told him I found two answers for his analogy. Either the perfect cereal doesn't exist or, if the perfect cereal does exist, I do not possess the means to find it."

"That would be how I understand postmodernism," replies Jason.

"Yes," I agree. "But McCleaver took the analogy one step further."

"How?" inserts Salome now interested in our discussion.

I turn to Salome. "McCleaver raised a third possibility. The perfect cereal does exist, but it had been removed from the cereal aisle before I got to the store."

"Translated, that means an absolute truth exists, but it has been removed from the public square to be forgotten," adds Jason.

"Professor McCleaver told me that Professor Wadford refused to answer his question for just that reason," I affirm. "We've been taught that holding to an absolute truth is tantamount to claiming possession of a superior truth claim that all must accept as true and that is the way into judgmentalism, intolerance, tyranny, and racism. But Professor McCleaver told me that eliminating the absolute does not open the way to democracy, inclusion, and tolerance…"

"Nonsense!" bellows Salome as she shifts in her seat uncomfortably in anticipation of where Connor is taking the conversation. "He is trying to hold on to absolutes! Men make up absolutes to gain power! I've taken a number of courses in feminist studies and absolutes are synonymous with male power. Take marriage for example. Marriage is just an institution set up by men to gain power over women!"

Demetrius, who has been silent until now, interrupts. "There are a lot of historical precedents for your claims, Salome, but I think there are other reasons for marriage."

"Like what?" demands Salome.

"How about love?" offers Sean quietly so to lower the temperature of the discussion.

"There is no such thing as love!" retorts Salome, now red-faced. "What you call 'love' is just another form of male-dominance!"

"If that be the case, if marriage is just to give men power over women, then why have homosexuals fought for so long for the right to marry?" queries Demetrius.

Salome looks at Demetrius with fire in her eyes. "That is a homophobic question!"

"Not really. It's a valid question. What is 'homophobic' is the use of a slogan to avoid having to answer a serious question."

"What is the sexual orientation of your instructor?" questions Sean.

Salome turns toward Sean who is looking at her. "That is a sexist, homophobic question! I have many instructors!" she replies acidly.

"Roseanne Pseudomai is one of your instructors," returns Megan. "I know that she is lesbian."

"So, what of it!?" retorts Salome angrily.

Demetrius answers. "Lesbians are attracted to women; men are attracted to women. Perhaps your instructor sees men as competitors. That could be a reason for her 'men-as-power' argument."

Salome pushes back her chair and stands abruptly, glowering at the seated students. "Sexists!" she huffs. "Sexists and homophobes! All of you!" She steps back from the table and turns toward Megan who is seated next to her. "And you are too!"

Leaving her glass of beer half full, Salome storms from the table and out of the entrance to Wally's Pub. Megan slowly stands, steps behind Salome's chair, pushes it to the nearby table from where it was taken, returns to her chair, and sits down. We sit quietly waiting for the cloud of animosity to lift. Then Jason looks at me. "What next, Connor?"

"Allow me to restate. Professor McCleaver told me

that eliminating the absolute does not open the way to democracy, inclusion, and tolerance. Instead, it opens the way to establishing a false absolute more favorable to the wishes of an elite, and which, by the way, leads to another form of tyranny."

"That is where we ended our conversation on Friday evening," replies Jason. "Demetrius sees a dark parallel between Professor McCleaver's depiction of postmodernism and the past practices of communism in the former Soviet Union."

"Wow!" exclaims Sean. "I have never seen postmodernism in that light before."

"Demetrius and I had the same experience. It was like 'scales fell from our eyes'."

Then turning to me, Sean queries, "Anything else, Connor?"

"I pressed McCleaver on absolutes. He told me that a real absolute can only be given by an 'absolute-giver.'"

Sean follows. "Seems like an 'absolute-giver' would have to be someone whose knowledge is far above what the rest of us know; a perfect human perhaps. Or maybe there is a God!"

A few smirks vanish as I continue. "That's what I intend to find out."

---

At two o'clock on Thursday Professor McCleaver is sitting at his favorite booth with his coffee mug on the table in front of him.

"Welcome, Connor."

"Professor McCleaver."

"Where would you like to start today?"

"I've been thinking about the discussions during our past sessions. It seems to me that the promise of postmodernism is autonomy. If all is relative, I get to choose the truth claims that best suit me and live my life as I choose."

"Yes. Therein lies the promise of postmodernism, and therein lies the deception of postmodernism."

"What do you mean?"

"Now that you are a senior in college, how many truth claims are there from which you may make your selection?"

I ponder the question for a moment and answer.

"I think I see what you are getting at. There is only a subset of all possible truth claims available to me?"

"Only the subset of truth claims the teachers of postmodernism want you to know about and to select from. In other words, you are not autonomous. You are brainwashed!"

I am intimidated into silence.

Professor McCleaver changes the subject. "Okay. Do you remember where we left off Tuesday?"

"Yes. We briefly looked beyond someone who puts forth a truth claim to someone who puts forth an absolute truth."

"And what did we call the person who puts forward an absolute truth?"

"An absolute truth-giver?"

"As you look across the landscape of truth claim givers, who do you think might be a candidate for an absolute truth-giver?"

"Hmmm. I don't know. I can't think of anyone."

"Then the number of candidates for absolute-giver must be small, yes?

"I guess so."

"Therefore, an absolute-giver must be someone

who is operating above normal human agency, would it not?"

"I guess so."

"A 'someone' connected to a source of knowledge from above human agency?"

"I guess so."

"Someone who can download knowledge from a supernatural source?"

"I guess so."

"Connor. Science is the study of the natural world. If the source of an absolute truth is supernatural, science can't help us. That leaves philosophy as the means to find the source of an absolute truth. But postmodernism denies the existence of absolutes and that brings us back to the analogy of the perfect cereal. Science can't help us and philosophy won't help us. The perfect cereal has been removed from the shelf *a priori*."

With mouth agape I stare at Professor McCleaver as he finishes.

"You will not find the answer to the question regarding the source of an absolute anywhere on the campus of this university."

Professor McCleaver lifts his coffee mug to his lips. He takes what seems a long sip of coffee then leans back in his seat. All the while he stares at me. For a moment his eyes narrow as if he is in deep thought. Then he inquires. "Didn't you tell me that you are minoring in religion and philosophy?"

"No. I'm minoring in journalism, but I'm taking courses in religion and philosophy."

"Very well. What did your religion professors tell you about absolutes?"

"Well, nothing, really."

"Then what did your religion professors tell you about religion?"

"All religions, ancient and modern, are essentially the same. The promoters use fear to seek power over the gullible. They claim there are one or more supernatural powers that can cause trouble if not placated. They set up rules that must be followed and payments that must be made to gain the favor of the gods."

"Hmmm. You raise a question that must be answered."

"I do?"

"Yes. We agreed that an absolute would have to come from a Source or Sources other than human agency. How would the Source communicate the absolute to humanity?"

"I don't know. Perhaps through a prophet?"

"Or perhaps through a fortune teller. You just told me that your professors claim that all religions are essentially the same; that the promoters make up rules for the gullible to follow so to avoid the wrath of the 'gods.' How do we know whether the rules are from above-human agency and therefore are absolutes or whether the rules are inventions of human imagination and therefore, as false absolutes, are relative?"

Speechless, I stare at the old professor. He continues.

"It looks like your religion professors are offering us an easy path back into postmodernism. We will have to revisit this question: 'How do we know whether the truth claims put forth by religious prophets are really from a non-human agency?' But for now, I want to learn more about what you came to understand about religion."

The professor pauses for another sip of

coffee. "Did your religion professors promote any particular religion?"

"No. I don't think so."

"Did your religion professors go out of their way to tear down or otherwise render unappealing any particular religion?"

"Yes. Several were outwardly critical of Christianity."

"Why do you think they were critical of Christianity?"

"Well, a lot of people in America identify as Christians, so it is the religion most are familiar with."

Professor McCleaver lifts his left hand to his chin and his eyes narrow. After some thought, he replies. "Perhaps that is the reason why your professors were critical of Christianity. Then again, perhaps not. Hmmm. In what ways were your professors critical of Christianity?"

"Well, Jesus never rose from the dead; miracles never happened; the Bible is full of errors."

With his hand still on his chin, McCleaver ponders. "Hmmm. Jesus never rose from the dead; miracles never happened; the Bible is full of errors. Hmmm.

Which criticism most impacted you?"

"The Bible is full of errors."

"Why that one?"

"We know the world is ancient, not six thousand years old. Darwin disproves Adam and Eve. Life originated through eons long evolutionary processes."

Professor McCleaver's eyes fix on me and narrow. "Hmmm. Connor, I think we're on to something here. Postmodernism is a framework for how to live in today's world. Oftentimes the promotion of a new framework involves the discrediting of an existing framework. Religion promotes the absolute. Postmodernism denies the absolute. Therefore, proponents of postmodernism within all disciplines must discredit religion in general and, as you say, Christianity in particular, if they are to abolish the absolute. Hmmm. Not only must they abolish the absolute, they must abolish the 'absolute-giver.' They would accomplish that by creating an alternative narrative."

"What would that narrative be?

"Perhaps you just stated it. The world is ancient, life originated through eons long evolutionary processes, there was no perfect world. This same narrative was put forth centuries ago by modernists who thought they could discover a new absolute through reason and science. They failed. However, postmodernists find the same narrative useful for promoting their message."

Now smiling, Professor McCleaver leans forward and holds up his coffee mug. "Connor, it seems like the conflict between postmodern theory and the absolute reduces to a conflict between narratives. What would happen if the postmodern narrative was shown to be fatally flawed?"

"Gee, I never thought about that."

"Next time let's take a closer look at the postmodern narrative. Shall we meet here again next Tuesday? Bring along your general biology textbook."

CHAPTER 6

# SESSION FOUR: POSTMODERN DOMINO

At two o'clock the following Tuesday I enter the Student Union. Professor McCleaver is back at his favorite booth.

"Welcome, Connor."

"Professor McCleaver."

"I see you have brought your general biology textbook. Hand it to me. Today we dismantle the postmodernist narrative."

The professor takes the textbook, turns to the page of contents, and thumbs down until he finds the chapter he is looking for. He looks up to me and speaks. "Connor, as we discussed during our last session, the postmodernist narrative rests on a string of propositions. Each proposition can be considered as a domino. Tip over one domino and the rest fall with it."

Then he turns about a third of the way into the book, holds it up, and turns it around so that the page faces me. "Can you identify this apparatus?"

"Yes. That's the apparatus Stanley Miller used to discover the basic building blocks of life. It's heralded as one of the great steps forward in prebiotic chemistry. It shows that organic compounds can be formed in natural environments apart from living organisms. We now have observations of organic chemicals in meteorites, proof that basic building blocks for life exist in outer space."

"You are familiar with the Oparin-Haldane hypothesis?"

"Yes, the Oparin-Haldane hypothesis lays out the chemical evolutionary steps from simple organic 'soup' to living cells. The Miller-Urey experiment proved the existence of the first step."

Professor McCleaver leafs through the next twenty pages of the textbook. Then he looks up at me. "On perusing the remainder of this chapter, I find no references to proofs for the remaining steps of the Oparin-Haldane hypothesis. Why is that?"

I stare at the professor. I have no answer for his question. He continues. "Connor, the Miller-Urey experiment was conducted in 1952. That's about seventy years ago. According to your textbook, there has been no progress in the field of prebiotic evolution since then. I submit that it is certainly not for lack of trying."

Still looking at me, Professor McCleaver closes the textbook and places it on the table. He continues more forcefully. "Stanley Miller was a graduate student and this work was done as part of his doctoral dissertation. Rest assured that what did not happen was that Miller and Urey sat down and figured out what the earth's primordial atmosphere must have been and then conducted the experiment. Rest assured that what they did do, was rerun the experiment using numerous combinations of gases until they found a combination that produced the organic compounds they were looking for. That single combination was a mix of methane, hydrogen, and ammonia."

Professor McCleaver leans back in his chair and

sips coffee from his mug. Then he finishes. "Since Miller and Urey were seeking scientific validation for the Oparin-Haldane hypothesis, they asserted that the mix of chemicals that worked must have been the composition of the primordial atmosphere. Why? Because that mix gave them the answer they were seeking."

He pauses to take another sip of coffee. "However, regardless of motives, the experiment was still good science."

I am surprised by his statement. "What to you mean by 'good science'?"

"Any worthwhile theory makes predictions. Miller and Urey made a prediction that the atmosphere of the primordial earth consisted of three gases - methane, hydrogen, and ammonia. That prediction could be tested. Geologists know that the chemistry of rocks is linked to the chemistry of the atmosphere. In order to confirm Miller and Urey's prediction, all they had to do was to test the composition of ancient rocks."

I am beginning to understand where Professor McCleaver is taking his argument. "They didn't find the predicted chemistry of the rocks, did they?"

"Remember now, the Miller-Urey experiment was conducted in 1952. Back then, the means to date rocks radiometrically was still in its infancy. Geologists were still searching for the oldest rocks. When the rocks they found did not have the predicted chemistry, the biologists claimed the rocks were not old enough. Furthermore, they claimed that rocks with the predicted chemistry had likely been subducted into the earth's mantle by continental plate tectonics and therefore were lost to scientific inquiry. But by the mid-1970s, geologists had found rocks that dated back to the primordial times..."

I complete the sentence, "...and the chemistry of the rocks was no different from rocks that formed much later?"

Professor McCleaver concludes, "Correct. And that means that the composition of the atmosphere has not significantly changed throughout geological time and that composition is not what Miller and Urey predicted. These findings led to the conclusion that life never originated on earth through prebiotic chemical evolution!"

"So that is why biologists believe life evolved

elsewhere in the universe and spread to earth," I offer.

"Why are we going to Mars?"

"To find evidence for life?"

"Precisely. However, there is a catch. Back in the early 1950s, about all we understood about the cell was that it consisted of two parts, an outer protoplasm and an inner nucleus. It was easy to imagine natural processes that could create something so simple. By the mid-1980s the science of biology had advanced to where we began to understand the extreme complexity of the living cell. Two scientists, Sir Fred Hoyle and Chandra Wickramasinghe, calculated the probability that the remaining steps of the Oparin-Haldane hypothesis could happen by chance. That probability is one in one followed by forty thousand zeroes."

Professor McCleaver stops to drink some coffee. "Back then I was an assistant professor just starting my career. After I read of the Hoyle-Wickramasinghe results I decided to find out just how big the number one followed by forty thousand zeroes really is. Connor, do you know how small electrons are?"

"Yes."

"I decided to pack the universe with electrons. I

imagined a sphere one hundred billion light years in diameter and packed it solidly with electrons. Then, because evolution also takes place over time as well as over space, I flushed out the electrons and repacked the universe with new electrons, doing this one hundred billion times a second for one hundred billion years. Do you think the total number of electrons exceeds the number one followed by forty thousand zeroes?"

"I don't know. It seems so."

With his eyes focused on me and leaning forward in his seat, Professor McCleaver concludes. "It turns out that the total number of electrons is one followed by one hundred fifty-two zeroes. This number is immense. To my knowledge, no computer has ever processed numbers this large. But compared with one followed by forty thousand zeroes, the number one followed by one hundred fifty-two zeroes is so small as to be zero, if zero has any meaning. Connor, prebiotic chemical evolution never happened! Anywhere!"

I am astonished. I stare at Professor McCleaver for a moment. A feeling of unbelief rises within. Then the feeling slowly turns to anger. "Professor McCleaver, I feel as if I have been lied to."

I continue staring at the old professor. "Problem is, I can't figure out who is doing the lying, you or the whole academic community!"

Professor McCleaver concludes. "If prebiotic evolution never happened, there remains only one alternative - the perfect cereal. We must face the prospect of a Creator! We are faced with the existence of an 'absolute-giver' and therefore with the existence of an absolute. With the collapse of the lynchpin of naturalistic evolution, the entire postmodern narrative collapses. Postmodernism collapses. If one domino falls, they all fall."

I continue staring at Professor McCleaver while trying to collect my thoughts. Finally, I think of a defense. Speaking slowly, I reply. "If, as you say, the theory of prebiotic evolution has been disproven, then why is it in my textbook? Why is it still being taught as a scientific theory?"

The professor leans forward in his seat and looks at me firmly. "By the late 1970s, geologists had shown that prebiotic evolution could never have happened on earth. By the mid-1980s, mathematicians had shown that prebiotic evolution could never have happened anywhere in this universe. Connor, the reason why prebiotic chemical evolution is still being taught is that no plausible naturalistic scientific theory for getting life from nonlife has been raised up to replace it."

McCleaver leans back into his seat and relaxes as he finishes. "You have undoubtedly seen science videos, documentaries about the atmospheres of other planets and moons. If evidence for water is found, there are almost always speculations regarding the existence of life, as if there is a simple formula - the presence of water equals the presence of life. These commentators are just propagandists for a theory that was disproven long ago. They work to convince the public to believe in an illusion, to believe the postmodernist narrative. What would happen if the public was told the truth, that the modernists and postmodernists have failed, and that we are faced with the existence of a Creator, possibly a Creator who is a giver of absolutes?"

I sit in stunned silence. Finally, after a long pause, Professor McCleaver finishes. "Connor, it seems you have some issues to think through. I will be here Thursday at the same time. When you come, please bring your Bible. We will spend our time taking shots at the other side."

"I don't have a Bible."

"One was not assigned for any of your religion classes?"

"No. We had a textbook."

"Well, you will have to purchase a Bible."

I depart the Student Union in a state of shock. Until now, part of me had thought of the old professor and his unconventional ideas as a form of semi-humorous entertainment. Not anymore.

After class Wednesday afternoon I go to the university library, search under Hoyle-Wickramasinghe, and find their book. Their calculations are just as Professor McCleaver had claimed. Then I search geology trade journals and, after spending a great deal of effort, I find references to the debate over the chemistry of ancient rocks.

I am a little late joining my group at Wally's Pub. The usual suspects are all present when I take my seat. After I order my meal, I stare at the tabletop like a zombie. Megan breaks the silence. "Connor, you look harried. Did someone run you through the wringer?"

I look up to see four faces staring at me. "Yes, I had

another session with Professor McCleaver."

"Wasn't that yesterday?" queries Megan. "That was Tuesday. What did he say that has you in a funk by the end of Wednesday?"

"That's right," adds Jason. "You two were going to discuss absolutes and the possible existence of an 'absolute-giver.'"

I answer slowly. "McCleaver destroyed postmodernism."

"What!? How did he do that?"

"He disproved the Oparin-Haldane hypothesis."

"The what?" questions Megan.

"The theory that life originated in some primordial organic soup," replies Sean.

"Hold on!" exclaims Megan. "What does all this have to do with demolishing postmodernism?"

"Megan," I reply, "postmodernism rests on the presupposition that that there exist no absolutes. That means there exist no 'absolute-givers.' That translates to man's being the highest order of life."

"In other words, man created himself through evolutionary processes, there is no Creator, there is no God, there are no absolutes." interjects Demetrius.

"Exactly," I reply. "All life is understood as having originated by undirected natural processes. That's why there is no real 'truth,' just 'truth claims' from human thinkers."

"This is all silly to me!" exclaims Megan. "I've never believed that life originated on earth. I have been told that intelligent life evolved elsewhere in the universe, and earth was 'seeded' by living organisms, perhaps bacteria in trash left behind by space travelers."

"That argument doesn't work either," I reply, still in a funk. "Professor McCleaver told me about research showing that the mathematical probability of the first living cell having evolved anywhere in the universe by prebiotic processes is zero."

"It's worse than that," adds Sean as all turn toward him. "I recently read that in 2015 three scientists won the Nobel Prize in Chemistry for decades of research into DNA. They found that DNA is an inherently unstable molecule. That means that, not only did DNA have to evolve from the primordial soup, but the cellular machinery to repair DNA had to evolve independently at the same place at the same time."

"The problem of the chicken and the egg,"

mutters Demetrius.

"What all this means," I conclude, "is that if prebiotic evolution didn't happen, then the origin of life by naturalistic processes didn't happen, and if the origin of life by naturalistic processes didn't happen, life on earth or anywhere else in the universe had to have originated through creation."

Sean finishes the thought. "And that means there has to be a Creator, and that means there is the real possibility of an absolute, and that means postmodernism along with all reasoning based on it are firmly founded on pure air!"

"Exactly. It's like a row of dominoes. Tip over one and the rest fall with it."

Megan asks, "Connor, are you planning to meet again with Professor McCleaver tomorrow?"

"Yes."

"What are you going to talk about?"

"He assigned me to bring a Bible to our next session. I guess we are going to start looking for a Creator."

"The Bible! The Bible is full of errors. It's a fairy tale!"

"That's what we have been taught," interrupts Jason. "Taught by the same people who sold us on postmodernism."

CHAPTER 7

# SESSION FIVE: BIBLICAL DOMINO

Approaching our meeting time on Thursday, I enter the Student Union holding my new Bible so that others can't see it. I feel as if I am walking to my own funeral. I ponder at the sight of Professor McCleaver sitting in his favorite booth in a corner of the faculty lounge. *Is he always alone? During all the times we have met here, no one has come to speak to him or even recognize him. It seems as if the University is waiting for him to die along with his ideas.*

Having collected my thoughts, I approach his booth.

"Professor McCleaver."

"Connor. Welcome back. I see you have brought

a Bible."

I lay my Bible on the table. Professor McCleaver produces one from the seat next to him and places it in front of him. "Connor, why don't we start with what you were taught in your religion classes about the Bible. Pick some issue that most interests you."

"After our session Tuesday, I thought more about why you chose to destroy the hypothesis for prebiotic chemical evolution. Naturalism hinges on a number of propositions. Discredit one and the rest fall like dominoes."

"Correct. I could have disproven other claims of postmodernism, but that would have taken longer, and would not have been as convincing."

"From what I was taught in my religion classes, I have come to see the Bible in the same way. Each piece of the Bible is a domino. Each piece claims to be telling the truth. Discredit one piece and the rest fall with it."

"Which part of the Bible do you see as the weakest and most easily disclaimed?"

"Genesis."

Professor McCleaver leans back in his seat and his

brow furrows as if he is remembering something from the past. Then he leans forward and begins. "Many years ago, when I was Chair of the department, I sat in on a lecture given by a visiting theologian. He began by stating that evolutionary science had changed the way we understood humanity. We once viewed our humanity as a little lower than the angels but, thanks to Darwin, now we view it as just a little higher than the apes. It follows that human life is not the crown of God's creation but the result of an intense survival struggle during the four and half to five billion years of our evolutionary history."

Professor McCleaver takes a sip of coffee and continues. "Once the theologian had put forth his opening premise, he proceeded to dismantle the book of Genesis and then the remainder of the biblical narrative. He argued that there never was a perfect or finished creation which God pronounced 'good.' If there was no finished and perfect creation at the dawn of history, then there could also have been no human fall into original sin. One cannot fall into sin if one has never lived in perfection. So, the mythical religious language of a finished creation, the fall, original sin, and the need for a rescuing God collapses. There is no need for Jesus as the divine rescuer, nor the story of the cross as the sacrifice designed to pay the price of sin."

Professor McCleaver takes another sip of coffee and concludes. "For those among us who accepted the theologian's premise it was easy to understand that the biblical narrative from beginning to end is all but nonsensical."

After a long silence I speak. "But you were never convinced of the theologian's premise?"

"No. I already knew that the Oparin-Haldane hypothesis had been demolished. That meant the theologian's opening statement was false and, as you say, that domino fell. Therefore, the remainder of his talk, though persuasive to those without a scientific background, was just a string of dominoes that fell along with his opening statement."

I had come to this session expecting to repay the old professor for his having uprooted my foundational beliefs in postmodernism and evolutionary science. I had thought that discrediting the Bible would be easy given what I had learned in my religion classes. Now I am not so sure.

Professor McCleaver continues. "If we are going to analyze a book, it is best to begin by looking at the author. What did your professors tell you about the authorship of Genesis?"

"Some said Moses assembled Genesis from a mix of written and oral material. One claimed that a later author, perhaps one of the prophets, or maybe an unknown source compiled Genesis from several ancient narratives."

"That would be the 'Documentary Hypothesis.'"

"Yes."

"The Documentary Hypothesis is a legacy hypothesis."

"What do you mean?"

"Theologians today who teach the Documentary Hypothesis were trained by their teachers who were trained by teachers and so on back almost one hundred years ago. That these teachers still promote the Documentary Hypothesis is a sign that they lack the mental energy necessary to keep up with the literature in their own fields of study."

Professor McCleaver looks at me firmly and exclaims. "Intellectual garbage! If the promoters of the

Documentary Hypothesis were really able to divide up Genesis according to nuances of language, then it would seem they would have had the intellectual fortitude to use the same methodology to determine whether the authors were or were not also writers of other parts of the Old Testament. And the act of assigning the authorship of documents that play such an important role in the history of a nation to unknown writers is an exercise in imbecility!"

Professor McCleaver exhales loudly in a huff, picks up his coffee mug and takes another sip. Then he concludes. "Connor, we cannot leave the identification of the authorship of Genesis to the unqualified. We will have to discover the true authorship for ourselves. Are you familiar with the word 'colophon'?"

"No."

"Go look up the definition. Then read Genesis and make note where in the text you find colophons. See you next Tuesday."

CHAPTER 8

# SESSION SIX: THIRTEEN BOOKS

I have the whole weekend to complete my assignment. On Tuesday at the appointed hour I enter the Student Union and proceed toward the faculty lounge. Professor McCleaver sits alertly in his booth. His Bible is prominently displayed next to his coffee mug. He sees me coming.

"Welcome, Connor."

I take my seat across from him and set my Bible on the table.

"Professor McCleaver."

"Did you finish your assignment?"

"Yes, I did. I found the definition for 'colophon' and read through Genesis noting where I found colophons."

"I need to stop you here," replies the old professor. "I am sure your reading raised lots of questions, but I want today's session to focus on the question of authorship. We cannot proceed to answer your other questions until we settle on who wrote Genesis."

I take a deep breath and exhale. Professor McCleaver continues. "Tell me the definition for 'colophon'."

"A notation placed in a book, usually at the end, giving facts about its production."

"What kind of facts?"

"Could be the name of the scribe who wrote the book, the name of the owner if the owner was not the scribe, the date the document was written, reasons for why the book was written, and so on."

"How many colophons did you find?"

"Thirteen for certain. Could have been more but the wording was obscure."

"Connor, according to the definition for 'colophon' as a notation placed in a book giving facts about its production, you have just told me that Genesis is composed of at least thirteen individual books or documents."

"You mean Genesis doesn't have an author?"

"Somebody cobbled together preexisting documents written by different authors. Genesis reads less like a 'book' and more like a 'compendium.' We now have a clue to help us unravel who that somebody was."

Professor McCleaver lifts his mug and sips coffee. Then he questions. "How did you determine whether the colophons fall at the beginning or at the end of the documents?"

"I started looking at the beginning. The first sentence, 'In the beginning God created the heavens and the earth,' reads more like a topic sentence than a colophon. So, I kept looking for the first colophon and found it at the second chapter, fourth verse. 'This is the account of the heavens and the earth when they were created, in the day that the Lord God made earth and heaven.' I checked to see if the colophon described the preceding events and it does. Then I followed the colophons on through Abraham about midway in the book."

"And then?"

"And then things got confusing. The pattern shifted. Colophons for Ishmael and Isaac clearly appear at the beginning of those documents. Same for Esau later in the text. But I had a problem when a colophon appears for Jacob after those for Ishmael and Isaac. That would seem to indicate that Jacob owned the document containing his biography as well as the information from Ishmael and Isaac."

"So, you found an abrupt change in the methodology for assembling the text. It seems your work has given us another clue to the identity of the redactor who assembled the documents into Genesis."

"How so?" I ask in confusion.

"It is possible the redactor changed the alcohol content of his evening drink midway through assembling Genesis. It is also possible that two different redactors assembled Genesis. I am thinking of Abraham and Joseph."

"What! None of my professors spoke of anyone before Moses and one even attributed the authorship to someone later than Moses."

Professor McCleaver stares at me momentarily then continues. "There may be other clues that will help us pin down the identity of the redactors. Genesis is an historical biography spread over a long family line. One possibility is that the redactor might have been inclined to edit out nominal events in the lives of his ancestors, while being inclined to include, in the narrative of his own life, an abundance of detail that would prove of little interest to future readers."

Professor McCleaver smiles then takes a sip of what must be cold coffee. Then he finishes. "Let's stop our work here. Your assignment will be to determine if I am correct regarding how the redactors recorded the biographical material of their ancestors and themselves. I will look into the education of Abraham and Joseph to see if they were up to the task of being redactors. Same time, same place Thursday?"

Late Wednesday I enter Wally's Pub to join Sean, Jason, and Demetrius. The four of us engage in small talk while we await the arrival of Megan. Jason has just told an off-color joke that has all of us laughing. Suddenly Jason's smile evaporates and his jaw drops.

"Are you kidding me? Here comes Megan and you won't believe who is with her."

We all look around to see Megan entering the pub with Salome. Megan pulls an empty chair from a nearby table for Salome and they both sit down. Sean exclaims. "Wow! Welcome back, Salome. We didn't expect to see you again."

Salome produces a small smile. "I apologize for the statements I made when I left. I was really angry. Since then, I have had time to think through the things I said and, more importantly, why I said them. Last Monday, Megan found me and we had coffee together. She explained that things for you have gotten worse, that Professor McCleaver demolished the foundation for postmodernism, and you are all reacting to that in some way much like I felt."

"Consider me stunned and punch-drunk," replies Sean.

I answer, "Initially I was angry with McCleaver and told him so. I told him either the whole world was wrong or he was wrong!"

"What was his reply?" queries Salome.

"He told me that I had some issues to think

through and he would see me the next session."

Demetrius holds his fist below his mouth. "Speak into the microphone, Mister Broadinski. In what subject did you get your degree? I got my degree in 'getting it all wrong'!"

Laughter.

"Now that the tension has eased," smiles Jason, "why don't we let Connor throw the next punch?"

"As you might recall, Professor McCleaver told me to bring a Bible to the Thursday session. I figured he would tell me about God as creator and absolute-giver. But he didn't. He asked me some questions about my religion courses. I told him that each piece of the Bible is a domino claiming to be telling the truth. Discredit one piece and the rest fall with it."

I pause for a sip of beer. "McCleaver asked me which book of the Bible I thought is the weakest link. I told him that domino is Genesis, the first book of the Bible. It lays out the creation of living organisms."

"What was his reply?" asks Megan.

"He said that, if we are going to appropriately critique Genesis, then we would have to discover who the authors were. He assigned me to find the definition for 'colophon.' Then he told me to find all the places in Genesis where colophons appear."

Salome looks on with her brow furrowed. "What is a colophon?"

"A notation placed in a book, usually at the end, giving facts about its production."

"Fine," interrupts Jason. "But why do you need to know that?"

"A colophon identifies authorship. I found thirteen colophons in Genesis. That means Genesis is not a book written by someone but it is a collection of books and documents written by a number of authors and assembled into a compendium by someone."

"You mean Genesis has thirteen authors?" asks Megan. "Not necessarily. Some authors wrote several books."

"So, what's next?" questions Sean.

"I think McCleaver is trying to establish who the redactors were. After that, who knows? He has taken sharp turns. I already have intellectual whiplash."

Demetrius muses. "Yes, McCleaver has taken sharp turns. One, he invaded Connor's philosophy class and questioned postmodernism. Two, he exposed postmodernism as a path to tyranny. Three, by discrediting prebiotic evolution, he proved there must be a creator who could be an absolute-giver. Four, in search for an absolute-giver, he has taken Connor into the Bible. Five, using Connor's claim that Genesis is the weakest link, he is zeroing down on authorship. Who knows? Maybe once he has established authorship for all thirteen books, he will have Connor select which of these is the weakest link."

Megan looks puzzled. "I'm not going to understand this unless I read a Bible."

"I've never read the Bible," replies Salome.

"Me neither," adds Demetrius.

"My mother took me to church until I left for college," offers Jason. "I know a little about the book, but not enough to talk about stuff with confidence."

Sean ponders. "Maybe we don't need to buy a Bible, because we don't know how long Professor McCleaver will stay with it. Maybe we can share one for now."

"Okay," I reply. "I will bring mine next Wednesday. However, if you want to read it in detail, you will have to get your own copy."

CHAPTER 9

# SESSION SEVEN: ABRAHAM & JOSEPH

On Thursday I take my seat across from Professor McCleaver and set my Bible on the table.

"Professor McCleaver."

"Connor. Did you finish your assignment?"

"Yes, I did. I am surprised at how simple things become when one lets a document speak for itself."

"What did you find?"

"I counted the number of pages, rounded up, that contain the documents identified by the colophons. I broke Genesis into two sections, with the first running from the beginning through Abraham, and the second running from Isaac through the end of the book."

"What did you find for the first section?"

"There are eight colophons in the first section. This is how the associated documents break down. Creation – two pages, Adam – 4 pages, Noah – two pages, sons of Noah – four pages, sons of Noah – one page, Shem – one page, Terah – one page, and Abraham – 16 pages. That's about fifty-two percent of the text devoted to Abraham."

"So, you have eight documents and one of them, the last one, roughly accounts for fifty-two percent of the text. That seems to confirm the hypothesis that Abraham was the redactor of the first part of Genesis. He condensed the stories of his ancestors and expanded on his own."

"Yes."

"How about the second half of Genesis?"

"There are five colophons for the second half of the book. This is the breakdown by number of pages: Ishmael – one page, Isaac – 5 pages, Jacob – 12 pages, Esau – 2 pages, and Joseph – 22 pages. That's about fifty-two percent of the text devoted to Joseph."

"Hmmm. Our hypothesis that Joseph was the redactor of the second half of Genesis seems to be confirmed."

Professor McCleaver leans back in his seat and sips coffee from his mug. Then he continues. "Now for the education part. Let's look at Abraham. Abraham's father was Terah. Terah and Abraham departed Ur of the Chaldeans, which was part of an advanced civilization. On the one page identified by his colophon, Terah records the nine-generation genealogy from Shem to himself. Thus, Terah had access to those who were familiar with his family line. He recorded the number of years each ancestor lived before he sired his offspring then he stated the number of years the ancestor lived after having sired his offspring. All of this implies that Terah was familiar with words, numbers, and languages.

"As he was raised in an advanced civilization and having lived with the likes of his father, rest assured that Abraham was well-educated. Furthermore, Abraham had access to the ancient documents that had been passed down to Terah. So, we can conclude that Abraham could have been the redactor of the first half of Genesis, including his own life."

The old professor pauses for another sip of coffee

and continues. "Now, about Joseph. Different story from Abraham. His was the third generation from Abraham. He grew up in a tent surrounded by sheep and cattle, so it is likely he didn't have access to formal schooling as Abraham may have had."

McCleaver smiles. "Joseph was schooled at home. At seventeen he was sold into slavery by his brothers. Being bought by a man in Egypt, he quickly showed superior management skills and was put in charge of his master's house. Then he was falsely charged with sexual assault and put in prison. Again, Joseph's management skills led him to be put in charge of the prison. Finally, Joseph was given charge of the whole nation as he became the second highest power in Egypt. He successfully led Egypt through a seven-year drought. If Joseph possessed the skills to save Egypt during a time of catastrophe, he certainly possessed the skills to, at the very least, employ a scribe to transcribe his grandfather's, father's, and his own biographies into the latter half of Genesis."

I reply. "Add to his skills that Joseph' biography accounts for more than half of the text and that his was the last document in the book of Genesis."

"Yes. And it would be about four hundred years before Moses appeared in the book of Exodus. I think we can be comfortable with the idea that Abraham and Joseph were both redactors of the book of Genesis."

"What would have been Moses' contribution to Genesis?"

"He could have updated the text by adding then-current names for ancient cities and physical locations; he could have changed old names for God for then-current names; he could have added nuances to the text to make it easier to remember. If Joseph hadn't done it already, he could have transcribed textural material from clay tablets to papyrus scrolls."

Professor McCleaver sips more coffee. Then he looks back at me. "Connor, now that we agree that Abraham and Joseph were the redactors of a two-part compendium, where would you place the weakest dominoes in the book of Genesis?"

"I have two candidates, both in Abraham's part of the book. They are the seven-day period of creation and Noah's Flood."

"Of the two dominoes, which do you think is the easiest to tip over?"

"The Flood."

"Why?"

"I have two reasons. One involves the magnitude of the event and the other involves the timing of the event."

"And they are?"

"First, there is no geological evidence for a catastrophic worldwide flood. Second, if there was a worldwide flood, it certainly wouldn't have occurred at such a late date as Noah's life."

"Hmmm. You mean forty-five hundred years ago?"

Still saturated in evolutionary thought, I reply. "No. I am thinking that in the history of the evolution of modern man, Noah would have lived about fifty thousand years ago. That's too recent in geological history for the occurrence of a major event like the Flood."

"Well, then. Why don't we take a closer look at Noah's Flood the next time we meet? That would be next Tuesday, same time, same place."

On Sunday night I have dinner alone in my apartment. I become curious about Professor McCleaver's claim that one of the roles Moses could have played in the construction of the book of Genesis was that of updating the text by adding then-current names for ancient cities and physical locations.

I open my Bible and ponder. *Hmmm, the best chance of finding place-name changes would be in the most ancient part of the book. That would be in the part redacted by Abraham. Furthermore, if McCleaver is correct about the redactor's including details from his autobiography while editing out details from the documents of his predecessors, then I would most likely find place-name changes in the part of the narrative that documents Abraham's life. There are eight colophon sections. I will search for place-name changes and make a list like I did for the number of pages devoted to each colophon.*

I begin with the first verse and search through the narrative to the death of Abraham [Gen. 25:11]. I make the following list of place-name-changes.

- 'Bela (which is Zoar)' [Gen. 14:2]
- 'the valley of Siddim (that is, the Salt Sea)' [Gen.

14:3]
- 'En-mishpat (which is Kadesh)' [Gen. 14:7]
- 'Bela (which is Zoar)' [Gen. 14: 8]
- 'Beer-lahai-roi (behold it is between Kadesh and Bered)' [Gen. 16:14]
- 'Sarah died in Kirjath-arbe (the same is Hebron in the land of Canaan)' [Gen. 23:2]

The breakdown by colophons of where these place-name-changes are found is, Creation – 0, Adam – 0, Noah – 0, sons of Noah – 0, sons of Noah – 0, Shem – 0, Terah – 0, and Abraham – 6.

I continue searching for place-name changes in the part of Genesis redacted by Joseph. I find only one - 'Ephrath (which is Bethlehem)' [Gen. 35:19] – found in the document belonging to Jacob.

I sit back and relax while musing. *I postulated that Abraham's section, being the oldest redacted, would contain the most place-name changes. Abraham's section has six place-name changes compared to only one place-name change for Joseph's section. Abraham's autobiography accounts for roughly half of the text in his section. That means half of the place-name changes should be found in his biography. But, if McCleaver is correct about the redactor's including details from his autobiography while editing out details from the documents of his predecessors, then I would most likely find the place-name changes in the part of the narrative that documents Abraham's life. All six place-name changes fall in Abraham's life.*

*Hmmm. Thirteen documents written by diverse authors make up Genesis. Abraham redacted the first half of the book and Joseph redacted the second half. Then, four hundred years later, the documents came into Moses' possession. He likely redacted the whole book and inserted the place and name changes just as Professor McCleaver suggested.*

*So McCleaver has it correct again. And so do I.*

*I smile.*

CHAPTER 10

# SESSION EIGHT: DOMINO OF THE FLOOD

It's Tuesday approaching two o'clock and I am on my way to the Student Union. No longer embarrassed to carry my Bible since nobody else particularly cares, I enter the building and make my way to the faculty lounge. Professor McCleaver waits with his Bible on the table. I take my seat across from him and set my Bible in front of me.

"Professor McCleaver."

"Good afternoon, Connor."

He wastes no time getting started with today's session. "Last Thursday we discovered that Genesis is divided into two parts. We saw Abraham as the redactor of the first part and Joseph as the redactor of the second part. We also found that both redactors cobbled together documents created by other writers. I am referring to the colophons."

I nod in affirmation of his summary. He continues. "I also asked you where you would place the weakest dominoes in the book of Genesis. I believe you replied that the Flood was the weakest domino."

"Yes, and for two reasons. First, there is no geological evidence for a catastrophic worldwide flood, and second, if there was a worldwide flood, it wouldn't have occurred at such a late date as Noah's life."

"Let's hold on to these two objections for the time being. For now, let's look at descriptions and the consequences of the Flood. In other words, we seek to answer the question, 'What does the Bible tell us about the Flood?'"

Professor McCleaver lifts his coffee mug to his mouth and takes a number of sips as he prepares himself for a long session. He opens his Bible to Genesis and begins. "The first reference to the coming Flood event appears in Noah's document. This would be the document ending with the colophon: *'These* are the records of the Generations of Noah. Noah was a righteous man, blameless in his time; Noah walked with God. Noah became the father of three sons: Shem, Ham, and Japheth.'

"Noah's document records, 'The Lord said, "I will blot man whom I have created from the face of the land, from man to animals to creeping things and to birds of the sky..."' God's message to Noah appears again in the first document written by the Sons of Noah. Noah is understood to have been told by God that, 'The end of all flesh has come before Me; for the earth is filled with violence because of them; and behold, I am about to destroy them with the earth.'"

The old professor places his Bible on the table and looks at me. "Connor, God decreed an end to all land-life on earth. This means that the Flood event was a mass-extinction event. The event does not have to be global in coverage, but it must include all places inhabited by land life. By adding up the number of years in the genealogy found in Noah's document, I find that, from the time of the creation of Adam to the time of Noah, human life had been on the planet for over sixteen hundred and fifty years. That is plenty of time, given birds, animals, and creeping things, as well as man, for land life to have taken hold in most of the habitable places on the planet. Therefore, for all practical purposes, the mass extinction event was global."

"I can understand that. But my first objection is that there is no geological evidence for a global scale flood. Are you saying that the mass extinction event was a global flood?"

"Certainly the event that caused the Flood was global but that doesn't mean that floodwaters had to cover every inch of the planet. The take-away is that conditions were not survivable outside of the ark, whether in floodwaters or on dry ground. Therefore, animals inhabiting places that would not flood still would have had to have made their way to the ark in order to survive."

"It seems to me that passages in the document authored by the Sons of Noah claim that the Flood covered the highest mountains. That means the Flood had to be global."

"That would seem to be the case. Until one looks closely at the document. "I can think of three reasons why they should 'think' the flood was global. First, God told Noah that He was going to destroy land life from the whole earth and use a flood to do it, so it would be logical to assume that the flood he saw was the global cause of the extinction. Second, Noah and his family were adrift for seven months without sight of land. If it was raining or otherwise cloudy, visibility would not have been that good. Third, one of the sons reported that the 'waters prevailed fifteen cubits above the mountains.' Fifteen cubits was the draft of the ark. The ark didn't bump into anything until running aground in the mountains of Ararat after seven months. But that doesn't mean the ark floated over the highest mountains on Earth."

"The Sons of Noah claimed that it rained continuously over a period of forty days. Where would the moisture for all the rain come from?"

"Suppose the mass extinction event was caused by a very large asteroid. If the impact occurred over the oceans, then huge masses of water ejected into the atmosphere could account for the forty days and nights of rain. However, such an impact also could have created waves within the earth's mantle. As the waves spread out, the land mass split apart into large continent-sized slabs that rose and fell with the waves."

I think out loud. "The slabs that subsided would have been inundated had they sunk below sea level."

"Yes. And when undersea slabs rose, much water would have poured onto land that originally was above sea level. Whatever happened had to have been more than just a tidal wave because the water rose and subsided over a period of seven months, according to the Sons of Noah."

"It still seems the Bible passages in the Sons of Noah document claim that the Flood was global," I protest.

Professor McCleaver stops and his eyes narrow as if he is pondering. Then he looks directly at me. "Hmmm. Connor, we know that every continent on earth is covered with huge areas of sedimentary deposits. If the continental slabs were riding on waves within the mantle, it seems that they all would have descended below sea level at some time. So, the Flood could have been global, just not everywhere at the same time."

He picks up his coffee mug and sips for a few moments. Then he continues. "Connor, other details of the flood are written elsewhere in the documents produced by the Sons of Noah, and you can read those for yourself. Now I am going to turn to the aftermath of the Flood for additional evidence that the Flood event was a mass extinction event of global proportions."

He reaches down to his side and produces a sheet of paper which he places on the table and slides before me. It is covered with line bars of different lengths.

"Connor, on this paper I have plotted the genealogies from Noah's document (which is from before the Flood) and from Terah's document (which is from after the Flood). This diagram makes it easy to determine who was alive and when. The vertical line marks the flood.

All nine bars for Noah's genealogy are plotted to the left of the flood line and are shaded in light gray. Adam's is the bar at the top and Noah's bar spanning the Flood is in medium gray. Terah's nine-member genealogy is plotted in dark gray to the right of the flood line. Shem's bar is also in medium gray as his life spanned the Flood. Abrahams' bar appears at the bottom and is included for reference. Only Noah and his sons lived on both sides of the Flood.

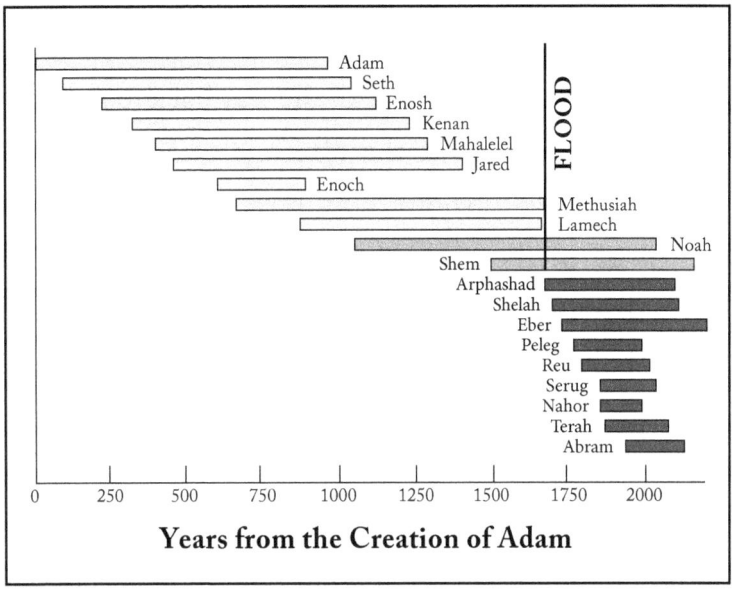

"Most of the lifespans given in Noah's genealogy range between nine hundred and a thousand years. This is the world God created. Methuselah lived to nine hundred sixty-nine years and died the year of the Flood. Noah lived to nine hundred fifty years. To see who lived contemporaneously with whom, drop a vertical line from one timeline to another. For example, Adam was still alive during the lifetime of Noah's father, Lamech."

I interrupt. "That means if Noah wanted genealogical information about his family line, all he had to do was talk with his father, who would have had first-hand information all the way back to Adam."

"Yes. Now look at the aftermath of the Flood. Terah's genealogy shows how lifespans decreased as men lived in the rubble of the world God created. Shem lived for six hundred years. The next three lived about four hundred forty years and the next three lived about two hundred fifty years. Abraham lived one hundred seventy-five years. Note that Noah was still alive during Abraham's lifetime. Shem outlived Abraham."

"Wow! Again, if Terah wanted information on the genealogy from Shem through himself, all he had to do was talk with Shem."

"Yes, if Terah and Shem lived in the same neighborhood. So, Connor, you have chosen a really big domino. The Bible describes two different worlds – the world God created and the rubble of the world God created. The boundary between these two worlds is the Flood of Noah. The Flood is not just a stand-alone story created by someone who wanted to produce an origins legend. The Flood is central to understanding biblical history. Tip over this domino and, indeed, all of the other dominoes of biblical history will fall with it."

I reply, "So this account tells us that we live in the rubble of the world God created, not the original world God created?"

"That's correct. If someone asks you to explain why God created a world with hurricanes, tornadoes, floods, droughts, earthquakes, and volcanoes, you can tell them that God didn't."

"Okay. I think you have offered a reasonable explanation for how the waters of the Flood could have covered the whole globe, but not necessarily at the same time. And I acknowledge that vast regions of all continents are covered with sedimentary deposits having been laid down over geological time. But I still maintain my second objection that there is no geological evidence for a catastrophe of this magnitude having occurred at such a late date as Noah's life."

"Perhaps we don't understand time. Let's pick this up again Thursday. When you come, bring along some current definitions for time. We will start from there."

CHAPTER 11

# SESSION NINE: TIME DEFINED

Late Wednesday afternoon, I make my way to Wally's Pub and join my friends. After a brief period of small-talk, Jason turns toward me and asks. "Connor, what transpired during your last two sessions with Professor McCleaver?"

I pull my Bible from my backpack, lay it on the table, and watch my companions. They all look at the book as if it is some kind of foreign object that should be touched only at one's own risk.

"Wow!" exclaims Demetrius. "So this is the book that was banned from my high school library!"

"I think I was in third grade when a school official came into my teacher's classroom and ordered her to remove one from her desk," follows Megan. "Said something about it 'corrupting our young minds.'"

"Corrupting us from what?" queries Salome.

I reply. "During our second session, Professor McCleaver posited an analogy about an *a priori* removal of the perfect cereal from the Walmart cereal aisle. Knowledge that all life on earth was created and that the creator might have framed an absolute was banned from anything we are taught. So that leaves us open to believe that there are no absolutes and that truth is relative, as is taught through postmodernism."

"The best ideas don't win if the best ideas are disallowed," mumbles Sean.

"If an absolute exists or if there is the possibility of an absolute," I follow, "then postmodernism and every thought system that links with it collapses. Removing the Bible from schools is one way of insuring that no one will ever discover an absolute."

"I want to know where McCleaver is taking us," declares Jason firmly.

All eyes turn back to me. "Remember our discussions last Wednesday? I think Demetrius got it right. Professor McCleaver established authorship for all thirteen books within Genesis. Then he had me select which of these is the weakest link."

"Which did you choose?" queries Sean.

"I chose the Flood of Noah because there is no evidence for such a catastrophe and, if there was, it wouldn't have occurred at such a late date as Noah's life."

Megan pulls the Bible towards herself while Salome looks on. "Connor, where is the account of Noah's Flood?"

Megan slides the Bible to me and I locate the beginning of the records for Noah's sons. "The text starts here in chapter six, verse eleven."

I slide the Bible back to Megan, who becomes consumed with reading and disconnects from our discussion.

"How did McCleaver answer your reasons?" asks Sean.

"Regarding my first objection, he claimed the Flood was a mass-extinction event. He postulated that a huge asteroid struck earth and devastated everything on a global scale. Nothing on land survived. The impact was so powerful that it set up waves within the earth's mantle. These waves broke the crust into continent-sized slabs, which rose and fell with the waves. Noah's ark was on a slab that subsided relative to the other slabs, and so it was inundated with water for seven months."

"I had been taught that the Flood was global," interrupts Jason.

"It could have been global but not necessarily everywhere at the same time. Furthermore, it didn't have to be global in order to accomplish the disaster God pronounced. That's what McCleaver thinks."

Jason turns to Sean. "Sean, do you believe this story?"

"When I studied paleontology, I learned that the dinosaurs were wiped out by what was believed to be an asteroid impact. That was a global event. But I've never read of anything like waves within the mantle. I suppose it could happen if the asteroid was large enough."

"There's more than just a flood story," I continue.

"What do you mean?" queries Jason.

I interrupt Megan's possession of my Bible long enough to extract from it a sheet of paper which I unfold and lay on the table.

"What is this?" questions Demetrius.

"This is Professor McCleaver's time-age diagram. It combines pre-flood Noah's genealogy with post-flood Terah's genealogy. The bars for Noah's genealogy are shaded in light gray and Terah's genealogy is shaded in dark gray, that is, except for Noah and Shem whose lives spanned the Flood. Their bars are medium gray. The positions of the age bars make it easy to determine who was alive and when, relative to others. The vertical line marks the flood."

I give each person time to study the diagram and then pass it on to the next one. Even Megan interrupts her reading to look. I continue. "The combined genealogy runs from the first man, Adam, to Abraham. Probably the major takeaway is that the diagram describes two different worlds. Before the Flood people generally lived from between nine hundred and a thousand years. After the Flood, lifespans declined rapidly, so that by the time of Abraham, people were only living to about one hundred seventy-five years."

"Wow!" exclaims Salome. And we think eighty years is old!"

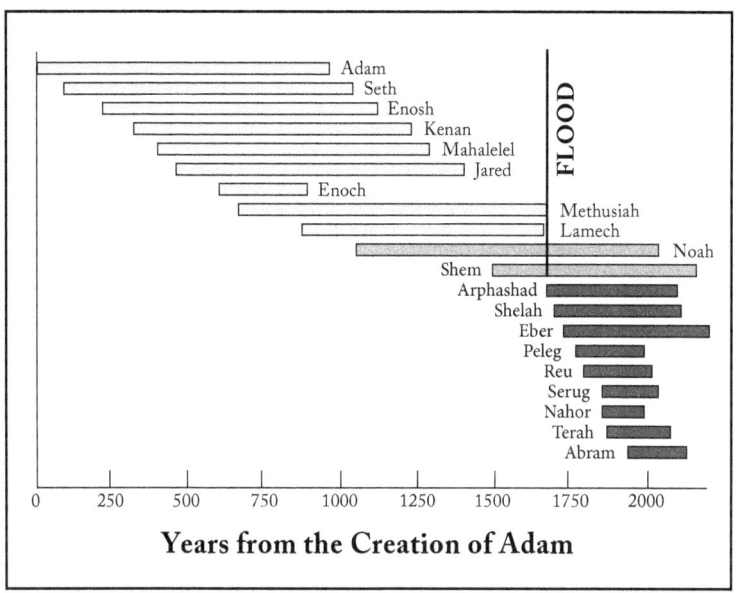

"Must have been some kind of utopian environment before the Flood. It was an event from which Earth has never recovered," I follow.

"If it's true," answers Demetrius.

"Point well taken," responds Sean. "Connor, I recall that you said your second objection to Noah's Flood regarded the timing of the event. How did Professor McCleaver respond to that?"

"He hasn't. We are going to take that up tomorrow." We finish our meal; I pry my Bible from Megan's hands, depart from Wally's Pub, and return to my apartment.

At two o'clock on Thursday I take my seat across from Professor McCleaver.

"Professor McCleaver."

"Good afternoon, Connor."

He sips coffee from his familiar mug. "On Tuesday we established that the Flood of Noah was not just an anecdotal story, but was, and is, a major domino in the biblical narrative. But because all the continents are covered with sedimentary deposits laid down by Flood-scale events over geological time, I argue that your first objection is not sufficient to tip over the Flood domino."

"I can accept that."

"However, your objection that there is no geological evidence for an event like the Flood occurring at such a late date as Noah's life is sufficient to tip the Flood domino. Therefore, I am going to spend some time explaining a framework through which I can answer your objection."

The old professor looks up at me and smiles.

"Let's begin. How do we reconcile your objection with documents written by different authors, all of whom claimed to be eyewitnesses of the events they described, documents that catalog events surrounding a catastrophe that massively impacted human longevity?"

"Maybe we can't. Maybe we have to throw out the Bible because it is demonstrably wrong."

"That is what a lot of thinkers have done. But I believe that approach is too simple-minded. That is why I asked you to bring current definitions for time. We need to take a look at how we understand time."

Professor McCleaver sips from his coffee mug. "So, Connor, what did you find about time?"

"I searched through a number of dictionaries. Several defined time in the context of Einstein's theories of relativity, and I didn't consider these to be of much practical value. The remaining definitions are different, but similar in that they all refer to events in some way."

"What did you find?"

"I made a list of definitions.

1) The indefinite continued progress of existence and events in the past, present, and future regarded as a whole.
2) A nonspatial continuum that is measured in terms of events which succeed one another from past through present to future.
3) The system of those sequential relations that any event has to any other, as past, present, or future; indefinite and continuous duration regarded as that in which events succeed one another.
4) The progression of events from the past to the present into the future.
5) Time is the ongoing sequence of events taking place."

Professor McCleaver sips from his coffee mug and leans back in his seat. "These definitions for time seem a little cryptic, don't they?"

"Frankly I was confused."

"I see two problems. First, not everyone experiences the same events. Second, those who do experience the same events do not necessarily experience them at the same time, or in the same way. Hmmm. From the definitions you have provided, it seems that time is not the same for everyone."

"So it's pretty hard to come up with a generalized definition based on specific events," I offer.

"One could argue that we really don't understand time. We need to explore these definitions in depth. Connor, these definitions are based on sequenced strings of events. We could call these 'chronological event strings.' If we know the intervals of time between these events, the chronological event strings become 'timelines.' So, the definitions we have for time are really definitions for timelines. My suspicion is we really don't understand time."

"Where do we go from here? Relativity-based definitions don't help much either."

"It looks like we will have to work with timelines. Hmmm. Every person has a unique timeline. If there are seven billion people living on earth right now, then there are in existence seven billion active timelines."

Professor McCleaver sips more coffee then looks directly at me. "This raises a question we have to answer. If we are to understand the meaning of time, don't we have to combine all seven billion timelines in some manner?"

"I don't know. Whenever I have read literature that includes timelines, there is always only one."

"Hmmm. Connor, I think this is where we should begin next Tuesday. All lives are interconnected in some manner. If we are going to understand time, I think we need to find a way to connect all of the timelines."

CHAPTER 12

# SESSION TEN: PIECE OF THE PUZZLE

At two o'clock on Tuesday I enter the Student Union and proceed toward the faculty lounge. The old professor did not give me any assignments, so I approach his booth with a feeling of confidence. Add to that a feeling of anticipation. The professor is going to do the talking and I am interested in how he plans to expand on the subject of timelines, especially if he thinks he can place Noah's Flood in geological history. I take my seat across from him.

"Professor McCleaver."

"Good afternoon, Connor."

Professor McCleaver sips some coffee, then with

furrowed brow looks directly at me. "Connor, we can't answer your question regarding the timing of the Flood until we have a better understanding of time. How can we combine multiple timelines to accomplish this?"

My confidence quickly dissipates. "Er, I don't know."

The professor looks at me sternly. "How can we understand the interrelationships among the timelines of many people if we cannot view them together?"

Still looking at me, he leans back in his seat with his forehead furrowed in thought. Then, leaning forward, he begins. "I think we should begin by taking a closer look at timelines. How do you see your personal timeline?"

"A line of events beginning at birth and continuing to the present."

"The present is just an infinitely thin boundary between the past and the future. Your real timeline extends from birth to death. Your current timeline extends from birth to the present. Your potential timeline extends from the present into the future to wherever it ends. I say 'potential' because your future timeline hasn't happened yet.

"When you were born, a subset of a near-infinite number of potential human timelines became available for you to live out. As you made decisions or, perhaps, as your parents made decisions that impacted your life, some of these potential timelines were passed by and lost forever. Think of yourself as climbing a tree of time. The past represents the trunk of the tree, a single line from birth to the present. Ahead of you, in the future, are all of the branches. Each branch represents a decision you will make, a decision that will lead to different events depending on which path of life you choose. Once the decision is made, the branch not chosen and its events are lost to you forever."

"So, as I age and climb higher into the tree, I make a decision when I encounter a branch. Then I cut off the branch I don't climb. The number of branches remaining as I climb becomes fewer until my potential timeline is just a single twig."

"Yes. Your timeline doesn't end at the present. Your timeline extends into the future all the way to death. Your final timeline will be one of perhaps thousands of potential timelines that are still available for you to live out. This is what makes the future uncertain. Your past is settled. There is only one timeline that defines your past."

Still looking at me, McCleaver sips more coffee. "Let's see if we can gain some more insight on timelines through a simple analogy. Suppose two men, Jon and Jim, are traveling to a small city called Flatville. Jim is following Jon's truck in his SUV. Upon reaching the west edge of Flatville at dusk, they pull into a rest stop. Just ahead the road splits, with the main road going on through the center of town and a truck route bypassing most of the city. They decide to separate, with Jon driving on through town and Jim taking the bypass. They plan to meet at a rest stop where the roads merge on the east side of Flatville and tell of their travels through town."

The professor pauses for another sip of coffee. Then he continues. "When Jon and Jim approached the city, they were essentially sharing the same timeline that is, experiencing the same events at the same time. Now they are parting to go separate ways and their timelines will separate with them. What do you think is going to happen?"

"They will experience different events."

"Yes. Jon drives through pleasant neighborhoods and comes to downtown - the life of the city. Lighted store fronts are filled with merchandise and people crowd the streets. Lights strung through small trees lining the curbs give a festive atmosphere. There are outdoor cafes and music flows from several venues.

"Meanwhile, the bypass takes Jim through a derelict part of town. Weeds grow along bent and broken fences. Stores with barred windows are dark. A few lights struggle through shuddered windows of houses. Small groups of people assemble beneath the few street lights while others prefer the shadows at the entrances to abandoned storefronts.

"As planned, they meet at the rest stop at the east edge of the city. Jim is astonished to hear Jon's glowing description of his travel through the center of Flatville. Jon finds Jim's account of his trip through the derelict community along the bypass almost beyond belief."

Professor McCleaver stops to take another sip of coffee. Then he continues. "Connor, you said that these two drivers would experience different events and so they did. In fact, these events were so different they could not be reconciled, that is, somehow interpreted through the other driver's timeline. No events on Jim's timeline could be used to explain the events experienced by Jon, and vice versa. Yet all of these events were equally credible."

Professor McCleaver stops for another sip of coffee. "So, Connor, what do these timelines have in common?"

"Nothing. The events encountered were so different that the timelines could not be reconciled. You made a point of that."

"Okay. Let's look at this from another perspective. Consider that the population of Flatville is several thousand souls. Thus, several thousand personal timelines were active when Jon and Jim traveled through the city. Do you see anything that is the same among the thousands of timelines?"

"No."

"My objective is to find a way to isolate Jon and Jim's timelines from the other timelines in the city. Do you see anything that separates Jon and Jim's timelines from the rest?"

"No. Well, er, yes. They experienced the rest stops in common."

"Correct. They were in the same rest stops at the same time. They held two events in common. So, the Jon and Jim analogy gives us a way to select their timelines from the total number of timelines found in Flatville."

"How so?"

"First, consider all of the timelines for individuals in Flatville. We can eliminate most of these if we retain only those timelines that pass through the first rest stop. We can further reduce this group of timelines by retaining only those timelines that pass through both rest stops."

I think out loud. "Hmmm. We can reduce the number of timelines still further."

"How so?"

"We now have only those Flatville timelines that passed through the two rest stops. We followed Jon and Jim from the west side rest stop to the east side rest stop. Other timelines that satisfy your criteria could have passed from the east side to the west side rest stops. Thus, you can further reduce the number of timelines by retaining only those that pass through the two rest stops in a specified order, say, from west to east."

"Very good, Connor. My objective is to select from all of the timelines in Flatville only those timelines that go from the west side rest stop to the east side rest stop. Let's define 'equivalence' as 'timelines that get us from the same beginning place to the same ending place'. Between these two common places, the timelines can pass through wholly different events as did Jon's and Jim's timelines."

"It seems to me that you could further reduce the number of timelines if you defined equivalence as 'timelines that get us from the same beginning place to the same ending place at the same time'."

Professor McCleaver lifts his hand to his chin and ponders. "Hmmm. We have to be careful with time. It is true that Jon and Jim left the first rest stop at the same time and that they were at the second rest stop together at the same time, but they may not have arrived at the second rest stop at the same time. We could be so restrictive in our definition that we inadvertently eliminate the timelines we desire to keep."

"Okay," I reply. "But won't you have to include

those timelines that satisfy the equivalence criteria at other times – from the time the rest stops were first constructed until the time the rest stops are torn down?"

"Yes, we will. There will exist a group of timelines that satisfy my equivalence definition. We will have to select the timelines for Jon and Jim from this group."

"Okay. Two timelines are equivalent if they get us from the same beginning place to the same ending place."

The old professor smiles as he reaches for a sheet of paper lying on the seat next to him. He hands it across the table to me. "Connor, I want to answer the question of whether we can combine timelines for multiple people. I have an assignment for you. I am going to increase the complexity of our study of timelines. This paper has information for events occurring on one day in the lives of three men, Tom, Dick, and Harry. Your assignment is to construct potential timelines for the three men."

I pick up the paper and peruse the list. "Doesn't look all that hard. See you on Thursday."

On Wednesday evening, I walk to Wally's Pub and join my friends. I am a little late and everyone else has already assembled. "Welcome, Connor," smiles Demetrius while others nod or lift a hand. I take the one remaining seat, survey the menu, and place my order.

"Hey, Connor," beckons Megan with a broad smile as she lifts from her lap a large book and slams it on the table with a thud loud enough to turn heads at nearby tables.

"What is this?" I query. "You bought a Bible? How far have you read?"

"Not far. Just Genesis from the beginning through the Flood. 'In the beginning, God created the heavens and the earth!'" she giggles.

"Find anything interesting?"

"Sure reads like God did all the creating during six days."

"Yep. I have yet to pin McCleaver down on that one. Anything else interesting?"

Megan opens her Bible to Genesis chapter five.

"There is an incredible amount of detail in these genealogies. Whoever wrote the first one…"

"That would be Noah," I interrupt.

"… would first state how long a person lived before he sired his son, then he would state how long that person lived after he sired his son, and finally he summed up the two time periods to get his lifespan. So, whoever, who, er, Noah, compiled this genealogy, knew how to add. He was a mathematician of sorts."

"If one is going to build an ark, he had better know how to take measurements," snorts Jason over his glass of beer.

The rest of us laugh at the sound Jason makes.

Sean changes the subject. "Connor, what's the latest from Professor McCleaver?"

After taking a moment to collect my thoughts, I reply. "Actually, I don't know for sure where the professor is taking me. We started with my providing a list of definitions for time. McCleaver claimed that we really don't know much about time because the definitions are not for time but for timelines."

Sean interjects. "I recall from our last gathering that you had told McCleaver there was no evidence for a mass-extinction catastrophe as late as five thousand years ago. Was that when he replied that we don't understand time?"

"Hold on!" interrupts Jason as we all turn to face him. "If we don't understand time, maybe five thousand years isn't five thousand years. Maybe five thousand years is five million years."

"He hasn't said that," I interrupt, as heads turn back to face me. "At least not yet."

"Then what has he told you?" questions Demetrius.

"Several things," I begin. "First, he claimed that every person, dead, living, or not yet born, has a personal timeline. For all of humanity, there exists a near-infinite number of personal timelines. Second, he talked about potential timelines."

"What are potential timelines?" queries Salome.

"Future timelines that are possible but haven't happened yet. That's what makes them 'potential'."

"I still don't understand what that means," follows Salome.

"Well, consider that you are about to make an important decision. Maybe you are deciding between staying at this university or transferring to another school. Suppose you are thinking ahead about what might happen, events that might occur, if you make one choice or the other. You are essentially imagining potential timelines."

"What else did McCleaver say?" asks Sean.

"He talked about timeline equivalence."

"What is that?" questions Megan.

"Timelines that have something in common, like they take you in different paths from one point to another point, as I understand it. McCleaver used as an example an analogy of two men at a rest stop on the edge of a city. One drives directly through town while the other takes a bypass. They meet at another rest stop on the opposite side of the city and discuss their experiences. So, what they had in common was driving between the two rest stops even though they went different ways."

"So what?" questions Demetrius. "What McCleaver is talking about doesn't make sense, or, at the very least, has no use."

"We have to keep all of this in its proper perspective," follows Sean. "McCleaver showed that prebiotic evolution never happened on this planet nor in this universe. That means we are created. There are no alternatives. There exists the possibility that the creator also gave some absolutes so postmodernism collapses along with all teachings that are based on it. The big question becomes, 'Who or what is the Creator?' It seems to me that McCleaver is pushing Connor toward the God of the Bible."

"The book that was banned from my high school library. Tsk, tsk," adds Demetrius.

"Why would Professor McCleaver push Connor toward the God of the Bible?" queries Salome. "There are other religions with their gods. Think of Allah and the Koran. What about Hinduism and its million gods? Perhaps ancient Greek or Roman gods. Or maybe Egyptian gods. Any or all of these gods could have put forth absolutes. So why would McCleaver push the God of the Bible? Is he a Christian?"

"In America that would be likely," follows Demetrius.

"Quite likely," adds Sean. "But that's too easy an answer. My experience with Professor McCleaver as my biology teacher is that his thoughts run deep. He has to have some reason for going with the God of the Bible."

"Well Connor, has the good Professor left you any clues?" questions Jason.

"Hmmm. Let me think. In one session he wanted to know what I had been taught in my religion classes. He asked if any of my religion professors had promoted any religion. I told him that I didn't think so. Then he asked me if any of my religion professors had disparaged any religion. I told him that some professors had belittled Christianity."

"How did he respond to that?"

"He didn't. Well, he did in a way. I gave him Demetrius' 'America' answer. He seemed to accept that, but then changed his mind saying my instructors may have other reasons for disparaging Christianity. Then he changed the subject and asked me what I thought was the weakest part of the Bible. I told him 'Genesis' ."

"And that line of discussion brings us to where we are today?"

"Pretty much. But, wait! Now that I think of it, there is another clue."

I turn toward Salome. "A big clue! Salome, you are

correct. McCleaver also asked me what my religion professors taught about religion. They basically said, 'All religions are the same.' So, if one joins a religion, it doesn't matter which religion and therefore which god he chooses."

Salome smiles, "Any or all gods could put forth absolutes?"

"Yes, that's when McCleaver asked me how a god would inform humanity of an absolute."

"What was your answer?" questions Jason.

"I told him the god would likely communicate through a prophet of sorts."

"And his answer?"

"How about a fortune-teller?"

"What?!"

"I think I get it!" exclaims Demetrius as all turn to face him. "If a genuine prophet told us something, we might be inclined to believe him. But, if a fortune-teller told us something, we might be inclined to be a little skeptical."

"Yes," I reply as all turn back to me. "McCleaver questioned how one could know whether someone proclaiming an absolute got his information from a divine source or was just making it up."

"Only a truth claim?"

"Yes. The problem of communication takes us back to postmodernism. Everything is relative."

"So how did McCleaver reason his way out of this problem?" queries Sean.

"He didn't. He only told me that it was a question that merited deeper thought and that he would take it up at a later time."

"Let's make sure he does!" exclaims Jason.

With Jason's statement, the discussion winds down. Megan takes advantage of the silence to turn us back to timelines. She raises her voice. "Wait a minute! The biblical genealogies Connor provided us form a timeline. The events in the Bible I've read about from creation through the Flood also fall on the same timeline."

"Hold on!" exclaims Sean. "I think Megan is on to something."

"I am?" queries a smiling Megan with eyebrows raised.

"Yes. Professor McCleaver is a master of analogies. His questions to Connor are not random. He is way ahead of us. He knows what questions he wants to ask Connor. Through Connor's replies and through what he teaches, he is assembling pieces of a puzzle. His analogy of the perfect cereal is a piece. His trashing of prebiotic evolution is a piece. All the effort expended on the authorship of Genesis is a piece. The stuff about the Flood is a piece. Timeline equivalence is a piece. Unfortunately, there aren't enough pieces to recognize an image yet."

"Sean, please enlighten me as to why Megan's discovery that the events of the biblical Flood form a timeline is so important to your puzzle," requests Demetrius with his voice lowered to sound professorial.

"Sure. Connor rejects the biblical Flood story because there is no geological evidence for a recent flood. The geological record forms a timeline. As Megan points out, the biblical record forms a different timeline. McCleaver posits an analogy in which two men follow completely different timelines and..."

Jason interrupts. "Connor, is McCleaver trying to convince us that the geological and biblical timelines are equivalent?"

Sean turns back to me. "Where is the Professor

taking this?"

I reply, "McCleaver hasn't said anything about the biblical timeline being equivalent with anything. He seems more interested in figuring out how to link personal timelines. For our next session he gave me an assignment to graph the timelines for one day in the lives of three men."

"Men in the Bible?" asks Megan.

"No. Tom, Dick, and Harry."

"So, what does that tell us about timeline equivalence?" chuckles Demetrius.

"I don't know, but I will probably find out tomorrow."

CHAPTER 13

# SESSION ELEVEN: EVENT THEORY

I find a block of free time after departing Wally's Pub and pull Professor McCleaver's paper from my notebook to read. *Tom, Dick, and Harry are good friends. One morning they meet at a hardware store and plan their day. Tom is going home to do some repairs, eat lunch, and mow the yard. Then he will join Dick and Harry at the steak house for dinner. Dick is going to drive Harry to the doctor's office for an appointment, join Tom for lunch at Tom's house if the doctor is running late, and drive back to the doctor's office to get Harry. Then both of them will go fishing on a nearby lake, clean up at Harry's house, and join Tom at the steak house for dinner.*

*Ahhh,* I think to myself. *This looks like a case of*

*equivalent timelines.*

I read on. *Tom leaves the hardware store at 10:15 AM and arrives home at 10:45 AM. He will remain home until leaving for the steak house at 5:05 PM. While home, Tom will have lunch from 12:05 PM to 1:05 PM, do yard work from 1:05 PM through the afternoon and then leave for the steak house at 5:05 PM, arriving at 5:55 PM.*

*Dick and Harry intend to spend the day together. Dick transports Harry to the doctor's office, leaving the hardware store at 10:10 AM and arriving at the doctor's office at 10:55 AM in time for Harry's 11:00 AM appointment. It becomes apparent that the doctor is running late, so Dick leaves the doctor's office and travels to Tom's house to have lunch with him. Dick departs Tom's house at 12:55 PM to return to the doctor's office. Then both Dick and Harry go fishing, arriving at a nearby lake at 2:20 PM and departing for Harry's house at 4:10 PM. They depart Harry's house at 5:30 PM to meet Tom at the steak house at 6:10 PM.*

I place the paper on the desk and ponder. *The professor wants me to construct timelines for Tom, Dick, and Harry. He lists the events and also the intervals of time between the events.* I pull a clean sheet of paper from my notebook and begin constructing timelines.

At two o'clock on Thursday I enter the Student Union and proceed toward the faculty lounge carrying my notebook under my arm. The old professor is waiting for me with his usual coffee mug in front of him and a folder resting on the table beside the mug. I take my seat.

"Professor McCleaver."

"Good afternoon, Connor. What do you have to show me?"

I withdraw my paper with the three timeline diagrams for the three men from my notebook and place it on the table in front of the professor.

He picks it up, studies it, and nods favorably several times. Then he looks up at me. "Well done, Connor. I have two questions. First question: Are the three timelines equivalent?"

"Yes. The three men meet at the hardware store in the morning. That's one event they have in common. Then they meet again at the steakhouse in the evening. They have the two events in common and their timelines intersect the two events in the same order. So, yes, by our definition, all three timelines take different paths from the hardware store to the steakhouse and therefore are equivalent."

"Second question. Why didn't you combine the three men into a single diagram?"

"I couldn't. Not all of the events were common to the three men."

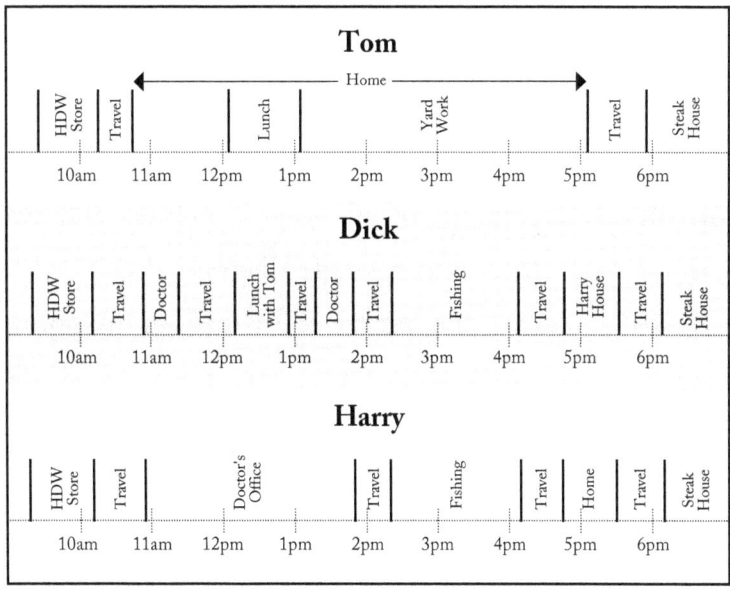

"That's correct. Then can we map the three timelines onto a single diagram?"

"We can't. We could do that only if all of the events

were common to all three men, they occurred in the same order and at the same time. In other words, we could map the three timelines into a single diagram only if the three men spent the whole day together."

"That's because we define time as a chronological string of events. Do you remember the definitions for time you gave me several sessions ago?"

"Yes. I recall that you said that the definitions were more for timelines than for time."

"Correct. We have locked ourselves into defining time by strings of events. By doing so, we make each timeline independent of all other timelines and we cannot map them into a single diagram. Let's break free by reversing the practice. Instead of mapping events into timelines, why not map timelines into events?"

"What do you mean?"

Professor McCleaver produces a blank sheet of paper. He draws irregular polygons in scattered fashion over the sheet. "Let's let these polygons represent the various events the men experienced."

Then, for each man, he draws lines connecting events in the order in which the events occurred. He finishes and slides the paper across the table to me. As I look at his diagram, Professor McCleaver explains. "The dashed line represents Tom's timeline, the solid line represents Dick's timeline, and the dotted line represents Harry's timeline. The interval of time between the events could be scaled to represent the travel time between events."

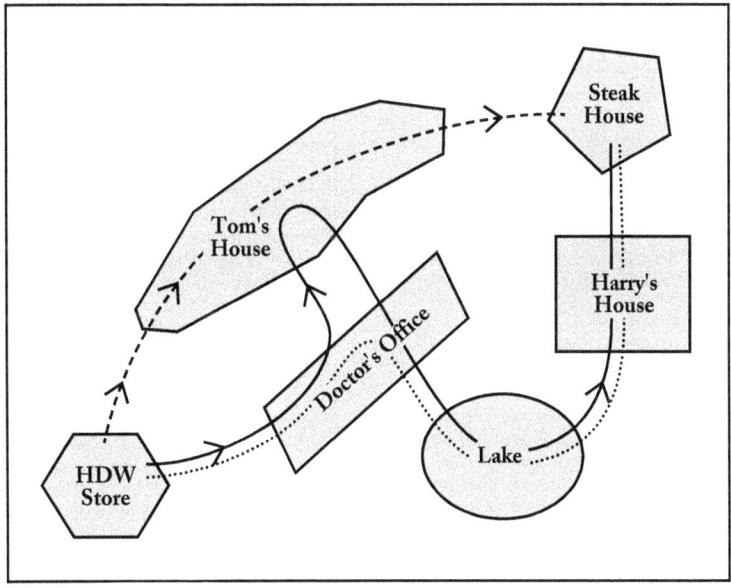

I study the professor's diagram. "Wow! It looks so simple."

The old professor looks at me firmly. "Connor, you are looking at more than a simple diagram. You are looking at a fundamentally different way to see time."

I stare at Professor McCleaver in astonishment. "Did you invent this approach?"

"I did," he answers with a smile. "I call it 'Event Theory.' Come next Tuesday and I will introduce you to some of the complexities of the theory."

CHAPTER 14

# SESSION TWELVE: RUNNING THE RACE

At the end of the session last Thursday Professor McCleaver made an astonishing statement. He claimed to be putting forth a fundamentally different way to understand time. He called it 'Event Theory.' As I rethought his event diagram, I saw nothing magical about it. He made no assumptions on which all subsequent arguments must rest. All the professor did was reverse the framework we use to understand the passage of time. Instead of ordering events over time to create timelines he ordered timelines over events. He only reversed the thinking. How could that be so profound?

As I approach the faculty lounge this Tuesday, I

see Professor McCleaver in his favorite booth with his coffee mug on the table in front of him. He seems lost in thought as he is reading over some printed material. He looks up momentarily as I sit down opposite him.

"Good afternoon, Connor."

"Professor McCleaver, what do you have for me today?"

There is a momentary silence as he finishes with his notes and places them into a folder on the table. "Connor, do you remember where we ended up last Thursday?"

"Sure do. You introduced me to 'Event Theory.' You mapped timelines for Tom, Dick, and Harry onto events."

"Did you notice that Tom, Dick, and Harry initially meet at the hardware store at the same time and finally meet at the steakhouse at the same time?

"Sure did. And since they start at a common place, live different lives, then end at a common place, I also noticed that their timelines are equivalent."

"Remember Jon and Jim and their trip through Flatville? They departed from the rest stop on the west side of town at the same time and, for all practical purposes, arrived at the rest stop on the east side of town at the same time. We noted that their timelines were equivalent and that the events encountered by both men were equally credible."

"Yes. You also showed that events along one timeline can be so different from events along another timeline that the events cannot be reconciled, that is, events from one timeline cannot be explained by events on the other even though the timelines are equivalent."

"So, the timelines passed through the common events used to define equivalency at essentially the same time in both cases. Now let's increase the complexity of event theory by looking at timelines that pass through common events at different times yet are still equivalent."

Professor McCleaver produces from his folder a sheet of clean paper and draws on it. "Here's another example of multiple timelines. Suppose there is a five mile long foot race. As with our previous example, all runners will have in common the beginning event, notably the start line, and the ending event, notably the finish line."

He draws two polygons connected by lines and continues. "Mapping the foot race might look like this."

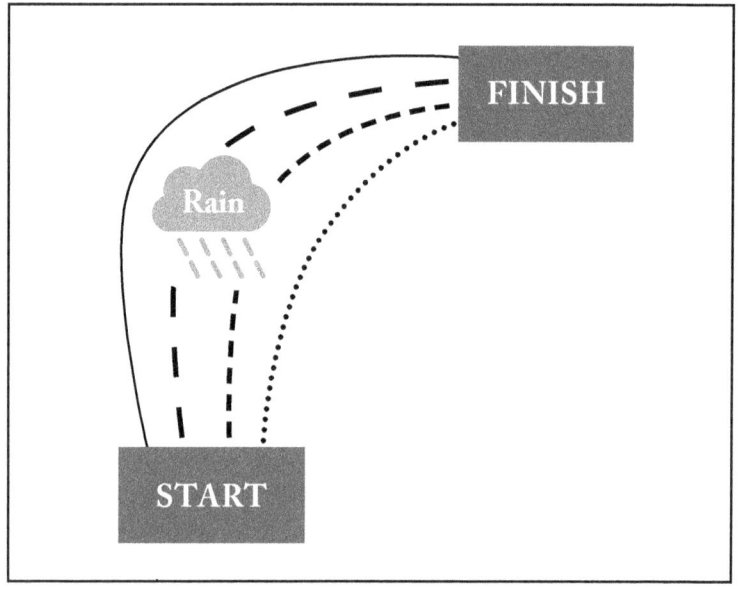

He hands me the drawing. "The length of the timeline is proportional to how long it takes for a runner to finish the race. Thus, the runner with the dotted timeline finishes first and the runner with the solid timeline finishes last. All runners begin the race at the same time. All runners pass the finish line – the ending event - but not at the same time."

The professor continues. "The simple message from Event Theory is this: It doesn't matter when a timeline passes through a common event, it only matters that it does."

"Hmmm," I ponder aloud. "Suppose I plan to go to the store today. My current location defines one specified event and the store defines the second specified event. There exist hundreds, perhaps thousands of equivalent potential timelines that will get me to the store. I could leave my apartment at different times and arrive at the store at different times and/or I could leave my apartment at one time but take many different pathways to the store, thus arriving at the store at different times."

"Yes. And there exist hundreds, perhaps thousands of different events for you to encounter depending on which potential timeline you take. Look at the foot race from this perspective. Instead of four different runners, let the lines represent four different potential timelines that exist for you depending on how fast you run. You would start at the same time but you would arrive at the finish event at different times."

Professor McCleaver stops to sip from his coffee mug. "But what if events change during the course of the race? Suppose a brief shower crosses the route during the race."

He places a gray polygon in the middle of the diagram. "The fastest runner (dotted timeline) passes the site before the shower begins. The next runner (small dashed timeline) passes the site just as it begins to rain. The later runner (large dashed timeline) passes the site during the heaviest rain. The slowest runner (solid timeline) passes the site after the shower has moved on."

"So, if I am a runner and choose which speed to run among the potential timelines, I can arrive at the finish line either dry or wet."

"Yes. This example shows us another interesting feature of Event Theory. I drew polygons as if they were fixed in time and space. Some events are but other events are not. The race route from start to finish is fixed. The rain event moves across the race route. So, depending on which potential timeline you choose, the same path can take you through rain or no rain."

Professor McCleaver pauses to sip from his coffee mug. "Here is another curious property of Event Theory. When the slowest runner (solid timeline) passes the site where the rain shower moved through, he finds the road is wet. Even though he does not experience the rain event, he does experience the wet road left behind by the rain event. The wetness on the road is not the rain event itself but is an aftermath or halo from the rain event."

"I don't understand."

"Perhaps we should stop here. Your assignment for Thursday is to bring a definition for the word 'halo'."

I am again the last of my group to arrive at Wally's Pub and I slump into the remaining chair. Heated conversation is ongoing. "I'm angry," expresses Salome who has been with the group long enough to feel sufficiently accepted to once again vent her feelings openly. "Problem is I don't know with whom to be angry."

Pointing at me she continues. "Maybe I should

be angry with Connor Wellington or perhaps with Professor McCleaver, who has twisted Connor. Because, without you two, I would be blithely living my life as I chose and doing the things I want. Except now I know that the choices available to me are not the full list of choices possible. Instead of feeling independent, I feel confined."

"You are becoming a critical thinker," returns Sean softly.

"Every problem has an infinite number of wrong answers," mutters Demetrius.

Salome turns toward him. "What?"

"Every problem has an infinite number of wrong answers. That is a mathematical truth. I thought the University is a place where scholars search out correct answers. Seems more like higher education has become a contest to see who can present wrong answers most eloquently."

"So how does that connect with what I just said?"

"I heard you say that you feel confined because now you know that the number of possible choices you could make has been limited by what you have been conditioned to believe. In my own words I am agreeing with you and adding that the subset of choices now available to you, thanks to the eloquence of the prophets of our culture, are most likely to be wrong. In other words, the correct course for your life may be outside of what you have been taught and therefore beyond what you know."

Jason interrupts. "Well, seeing that the source of Salome's discomfort has joined us, perhaps we can get some more answers, hopefully correct answers."

"Yes," follows Megan as she faces me. "Connor, what's the new answer? Has Professor McCleaver answered your objections about the timing of the Flood?"

"Not yet. But I think I know where he is going."

"Where?"

"A different way to look at time. Event Theory."

"Event Theory!? What is that? What does Event Theory have to do with the Bible?"

"At present, nothing. Remember the last time we met, I mentioned that I was assigned to supply McCleaver with a list of definitions for time. I gave him the list and he turned it down, saying that the definitions were not for time but for timelines and that we don't really understand time. Then he started talking about timelines and finished by giving me an assignment to map the activities of one day for three men, Tom, Dick, and Harry."

Sean and Jason nod in affirmation.

"I gave McCleaver three diagrams, one for each of the men's events. Then he asked me why I didn't map the activities of the three men into one diagram."

"That can't be done," interrupts Demetrius.

"True," follows Sean. "But not true if the three men share the same events."

"And at the same time," I correct.

Demetrius frowns. "Kind of a trivial case. Just put three names at the bottom of a diagram created for one person. So what?"

"What did McCleaver do?" queries Megan.

I pass around McCleaver's event diagram for Tom, Dick, and Harry. "Instead of mapping events into timelines, he mapped timelines into events."

"Wow! Cool!" exclaims Demetrius. "I get it!"

"What do you get?" questions Megan.

"There's no limit to the number of timelines that can be mapped into an event diagram. One could map all of history into a single diagram!"

"What does that accomplish?"

"Don't take my answer. The potential is open to the wildest of imaginations."

Jason raises his hand slightly to gain attention. "I would like Connor to proceed. Connor?"

"That was last Thursday. Yesterday, Professor McCleaver produced this diagram."

I pass around McCleaver's event diagram for the foot race. After each has had time to look over the diagram, I continue. "The point of this event diagram is that all runners depart the starting event at the same time and all runners pass through the finish event, but not at the same time. The first diagram starts with Tom, Dick, and Harry's timelines at the hardware store at the same time and ends with their timelines at the steak house at the same time. The second event diagram shows that timelines don't have to pass through the two common events at the same time to be equivalent."

"Hmmm," ponders Demetrius. "This goes beyond simply mapping timelines into events. This appears to be a new framework for understanding the chronology of events."

"How so?" queries Sean.

Demetrius ponders Sean's question. Then he replies. "We see our timelines as fixed with new events added over time. Your timeline is your frame of reference. McCleaver's Event Theory changes how we see our timelines. Events become the frames of reference."

Salome glowers at Demetrius. "It seems that you are the brilliant one in this group. I didn't understand a word of what you just said. Try explaining it for me."

"Okay. Do you drive a car?"

"Yes."

"Do you have your car serviced at the dealership?"

"Yes. Why to you ask?"

"Suppose you have your car serviced today. Having that job done is just one event on your timeline today. Correct?"

"Okay, I understand that."

"Now suppose when you walk into the service department, the manager comes up to you and says, 'Congratulations, Miss Kublish. You are our one-thousandth customer to come in this year. In recognition of this distinction, we will service your vehicle at no charge to you!'"

"I would like to see that happen," smiles Salome.

"My point is this: The servicing is just one event on your timeline. To the service manager, your timeline is the one-thousandth timeline to pass through the service event. For you, your timeline is the frame of reference; for the service manager, the service event is the frame of reference. For the service manager, it doesn't matter when a timeline passes through his event; it only matters that it does."

Jason gives Salome a moment to reply to Demetrius. When she doesn't, Jason turns toward me. "What's next with McCleaver?"

"We meet again tomorrow and Professor McCleaver is going to explain more of the complexities of his Event Theory. I hope."

CHAPTER 15

# SESSION THIRTEEN: ON HALOES

After class on Thursday morning, I seek out a dictionary and look up the word 'halo.' As I ponder the definitions for 'halo' it seems to me that my discussions with Professor McCleaver are getting further from the issue of Noah's Flood and its impossibility. I wonder whether I should continue with the biweekly meetings in the faculty lounge. But then I recall how the professor had demolished the theory of prebiotic evolution and set in motion the collapse of dominoes that made up my 'scientific' worldview. I would like to return the favor.

At two o'clock I enter the faculty lounge of the Student Union and proceed to the booth where

Professor McCleaver sits.

"Professor."

"Good afternoon, Connor. What did you find about haloes?"

"The definitions I found don't seem to have much relationship to wet roads."

"Go ahead."

"The dictionary I used defines 'halo' in two ways. First, a halo is a disk or circle of light shown surrounding or above the head of a saint or holy person to represent their holiness. Second, a halo is a circle of white or colored light around the sun, moon, or other luminous bodies, caused by refraction through ice crystals in the atmosphere."

The old professor raises his hand to his chin for a moment. Then he begins. "From the definitions you gave, notice that the halo itself is not of the same substance as the thing which causes it. For example, the halo surrounding the head of a holy person is not of itself holy, nor is it part of the holy person. The halo exists only because the saint exists, but it is not the saint. In the same way, the halo surrounding the moon exists because the moon exists and ice crystals refract light. But the halo is not part of the moon nor is the halo made of ice. Therefore, in the context of Event Theory, a 'halo' is some kind of residue, or byproduct, or after-effect of an event, but it is not the event itself."

Professor McCleaver pauses to sip some coffee. "Let me give some examples of what I intend 'halo' to mean. Suppose a beloved family member dies. Death is an event. Other family members suffer loss to some degree depending on their relationship to the deceased family member. Their losses are 'haloes' of the death but not the death itself."

"So," I reply, "thinking back to the foot race, the fourth runner encountered the wet road. The wetness was just the 'halo' of the shower."

"Correct. The rain event left the road wet but the wet road was not the rain event. The wet road was the 'halo' of the rain event. Suppose that when the fourth runner passed over the wet road, he noticed a fire truck parked nearby."

"He could easily misinterpret the reason for the wet road."

"Here's another example of haloes. Suppose a resident of Pensacola, Florida, spends a week in

Nashville, Tennessee. He returns to find his home devastated by a hurricane. The devastation is the 'halo' or aftermath of the hurricane but not the hurricane itself. Had he remained in Pensacola, he would have experienced both the event (hurricane) and its halo (aftermath). But his personal timeline shifted from Pensacola to Nashville then back to Pensacola, so he did not experience the event, but did experience the halo of the event."

Professor McCleaver stops for a sip of coffee. Then he looks directly at me. "Connor, this 'halo effect' can have profound impact thousands, millions, and even billions of years later on timelines that do not intersect with the original events. This is the most confusing property of Event Theory I have yet found."

"I'm glad to hear you say that. I am thoroughly confused, especially since I don't know how all this works out."

"There is one more property of Event Theory to explore and then we will be able to see how dominoes fall."

The old professor takes another sip of coffee and places his mug on the table in front of him. "That property is the heterogeneity of events. We have already noted that, relative to our timelines, some events are fixed while other events are in motion. With regard to heterogeneity, some timelines that intersect the same events may not be impacted in the same way.

"Let's return to the example of the foot race. Two of the runners experienced the same event – the rain shower. However, the first runner experienced the event as the rain began, but the second runner experienced the full deluge. The outcome was that both runners experienced the same rain event, but not in the same way.

"For another example, let's return to the homeowner in Pensacola who traveled to Nashville. The many residents who remained in Pensacola experienced the hurricane event. That does not mean everyone experienced the hurricane event in the same way or at the same time. Some residents experienced strong but non-devastating winds. Other residents suffered a brush with the eye wall. Still other residents experienced the calm of the hurricane's 'eye.'

"Hurricanes have distinct physical structures. Winds increase as one goes from the edge toward the center. Maximum winds are typically found in the eye wall surrounding the center. Then winds drop to near calm inside the eye wall. Thus, hurricanes, as events, are heterogeneous in space. Furthermore, hurricanes are heterogeneous in time. Hurricanes have a life-history, beginning as small disturbances, growing to maximum strength, and then diminishing to small disturbances. Thus, when and how one's timeline intersects with a hurricane event will determine the impact of the event and/or its halo on that person."

Professor McCleaver leans back in his seat. "So, Connor, you have been introduced to Event Theory. What have you learned so far?"

"Well, we began by defining time more in terms of timelines, the stringing together of events in the order they occur. You talked about potential timelines as timelines that could happen in the future. Then you changed the framework for understanding timelines. So, instead of seeing events happening over time, we see timelines flowing through a field of events. This change in perspective allows us to map the timelines of many people through a large number of events. You pointed out that events are heterogeneous, so two people may not experience the same event in the same way. And you introduced the concept of 'halo,' whereby a timeline may pass through the effect of an event but not the event itself."

"Very good, Connor. Now we are ready to knock over dominoes. See you next Tuesday."

CHAPTER 16

# SESSION FOURTEEN: TWO EQUIVALENT TIMELINES

On Tuesday I enter the Student Union and proceed toward the faculty lounge. With a sense of anticipation, I arrive at the booth where Professor McCleaver sits.

"Professor."

"Good afternoon, Connor. Are you ready to tip over dominoes?"

"Very ready."

"I am going to proceed toward answering your second objection to the Flood of Noah, that being that a Flood-scale event could not have occurred so late as during Noah's lifetime."

"Good. I think I have a valid objection that has

to be addressed if I am going to accept the possibility that Noah's Flood actually happened. Otherwise, I see the late date as tipping over Noah's domino."

"Very well. Let's move our discussion of events and timelines to a grander perspective. Imagine all events, significant and insignificant, natural and supernatural, that have occurred or will occur anywhere in the cosmos from the time of the big bang to the time of the heat death of the universe. Picture all of these events enclosed within a giant cube. Now imagine all of the potential timelines that could be mapped through the near-infinite number of potential events. What do you think you would see?"

"If each potential timeline is represented by a line, the cube would be packed solid by an infinite number of potential timelines."

"Correct. Let us reduce the number of potential timelines. Consider the foot race we discussed just two sessions ago. Only those potential timelines that represent runners were mapped. Timelines associated with spectators were ignored. The potential timelines of the runners passed through two events, the start event and the finish event in that order. In a similar way, we can further reduce the number of potential timelines found in the event cube by retaining only those that pass through specified starting and ending events. In other words, we will require the timelines we retain to be mutually equivalent. What do you think you would see now?"

I pause for a moment to think. Then I reply. "Hmmm. If the potential timelines that pass through the two specified events are free to go anywhere else, I think that the number of potential timelines passing through these two events is still near infinity."

"Correct."

Professor McCleaver pauses to sip more coffee. Then he opens a folder on the seat beside him, extracts a piece of paper, and slides it across the table to me. I pick up the paper and study the image. I see a diagram showing the outlines of a three-dimensional box with two lines, one solid and the other dashed, twisting within the box to connect two events 'B' and 'E.'

The professor continues. "The diagram shows two potential timelines selected from the near infinite number of possible equivalent potential timelines that pass through the two events. What can you tell me about these two potential timelines?"

"Well, the solid potential timeline is longer than the dashed potential timeline and, judging by the shapes of the lines, neither the solid line is the longest timeline nor is the dashed line the shortest timeline that could be drawn between the two events."

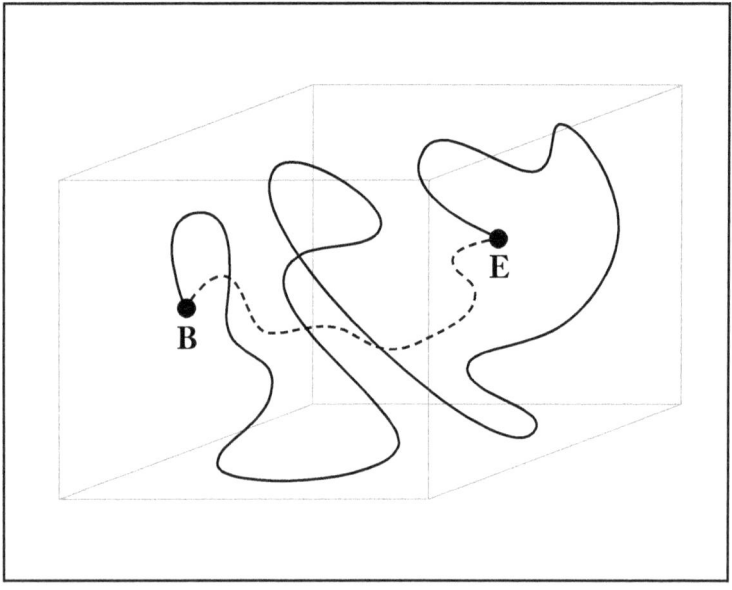

"Correct and correct. Anything else?"

"The potential timelines don't look like they are much related to each other except possibly near the common events where they come close together."

"Correct again. If the potential timelines are not related to each other, we can conclude that they pass through wholly different events, much like Jon and Jim's trips through Flatville.

Furthermore, just like the events encountered by Jon and Jim, the events encountered by the two timelines in the event cube are equally credible. Yes?"

"Yes."

I place the diagram on the table in front of me. "Okay. You've shown me a diagram of two potential timelines passing between two points. I take it that 'B' represents a 'beginning' event and 'E' represents an 'ending' event. That means the timelines are equivalent. What's special about this diagram?"

"It all depends on how I define 'B' and 'E.'"

I look at him blankly. He holds up the diagram so that I can see it. "Connor, suppose 'B' represents the beginning of Earth and 'E' represents the ending of Earth."

I freeze in my seat. I say nothing because I have nothing to say. I am astonished! Finally, I summon a sentence. "You are saying that there are two potential timelines passing through equally credible events. The solid line is the geological timeline and the dashed line is the biblical timeline?"

"I am saying that there exists an infinite number of equivalent potential timelines that pass though the two events. The geological timeline and the biblical timeline are the only potential timelines we know about."

"Well, just to say there are potential timelines and that they are equivalent, doesn't mean they are real timelines."

"Are you suggesting the geological timeline doesn't exist?"

"No, I'm suggesting the biblical timeline doesn't exist."

"That means you are claiming that, not only did the Flood of Noah not happen, the entirety of the biblical narrative did not happen."

"Not necessarily."

"Even Jesus Christ referred to the Flood as if the Flood actually happened. Accept all of it or accept none of it. If one domino falls, they all fall."

"Okay. But you will have to prove that both

timelines are equivalent. You will have to prove that they both actually pass through the same beginning and ending events."

"Fair enough. That will be the subject for our Thursday session."

On Wednesday I show up at Wally's Pub early enough so as not to be last to arrive. While we wait for Sean, I ask Megan a question.

"Megan, did you bring your Bible?"

"No! I didn't bring it because our discussions have gotten away from it. But I'm still reading my Bible and I have a question. Does God speak to humans?"

"How far have you gotten?"

"I've been reading about Abraham. It seems like God talks to Abraham all the time. Does that actually happen?"

Demetrius leans forward, his brow furrowed. "Are you thinking of 'back then' or 'now'?"

"I don't know. Could be both. Since Connor told us that mankind is created, I have been thinking of the creator as an impersonal force. Maybe something like the 'force' in Star Wars."

"Do you know the meaning of Christmas?" queries Jason.

Megan smiles. "Sure. Christmas is an end-of-the-year holiday when people exchange gifts."

"Christmas means 'Christ Mass,' which is a Catholic service celebrating the birth of Jesus Christ," follows Jason.

"Oh!"

"You may be correct in that the creator is an impersonal force. If so, then the creator is not the God that appears in the Bible."

"Okay. So, the God of the Bible is personal and talks to people like Abraham?"

Sean approaches the table. "Hi, gang. Sorry I am late but I needed to stay after class to discuss some questions with one of my professors."

After Sean places his order, Jason begins. "Now that everyone is present, let's hear from Connor about Event Theory."

As all faces turn toward me, I take a deep breath and begin.

"During the past two sessions, last Thursday and yesterday, Professor McCleaver fleshed out his Event Theory. His events are heterogeneous in both space and time. They appear and disappear and move relative to each other. Some events leave behind a residue of sorts. A timeline can pass through the residue, or 'halo' as McCleaver likes to call it, without passing through the event itself."

I place the diagram showing the two timelines on the table for all to see and continue. "But the real earth-shaker is this diagram. McCleaver started by asking me to picture all events, both real and imagined, from the big bang to the future heat death of the universe, contained within an enormous cube.

"If potential timelines were drawn to connect with all of the events, the total number of timelines would approach infinity. McCleaver simplified the problem by retaining only those that pass through two events, 'B' and 'E' meaning that only equivalent timelines remain. There still remains a near infinite number of potential timelines. Finally, he chose just two potential timelines as shown in the diagram."

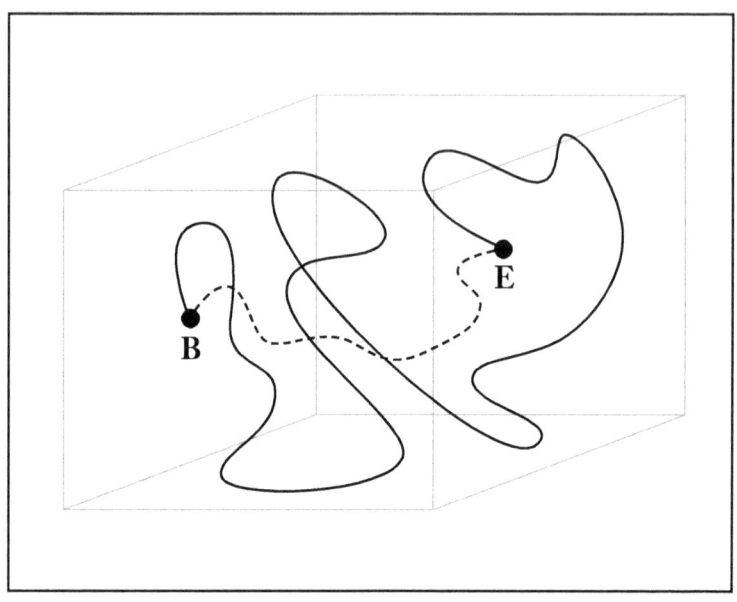

"Wow!" interrupts Demetrius. "It's just as I said when Connor first mentioned McCleaver's event theory! One could put all of history into one of these event diagrams."

"What's so important about these two potential timelines?" questions Jason.

I smile. "It depends on how I define 'B' and 'E'."

Sean expresses a slight frown and asks cautiously. "Okay, how did McCleaver define 'B' and 'E'?"

"'B' is the beginning of earth and 'E' is the ending of earth."

My statement is met with silence. Then Demetrius laughs. "Oh! Oh! I see a train wreck coming!"

Megan finishes. "Looks like I need to bring my Bible next time."

CHAPTER 17

# SESSION FIFTEEN: THE BEGINNING

Late Thursday morning I finish my classwork and find time to contemplate my last session with Professor McCleaver. *This all started when Professor McCleaver invaded Professor Wadford's lecture and challenged the basic presuppositions of postmodern thought. It was the first time in my four years at this university that postmodernism had been challenged. I followed Professor McCleaver out of curiosity and he invited me to discuss his ideas with him.*

I smile as I think of the professor's first session. *He took me into Walmart and showed me the cereal aisle. His assignment for me was to find the perfect cereal which, of course, I could not do. Then he told me it was possible that* the perfect cereal had been removed before we got to the market. Of course, he was just making an analogy with the marketplace of ideas. If there is an absolute, it must be removed from the marketplace of ideas before there can be the introduction of philosophies based on relativism. If the absolute reappears, then all philosophies based on relativism are demonstrably false. More importantly, if there is an absolute, there must be an absolute-giver.

That's why Professor McCleaver demolished prebiotic evolution. Life never generated from nonlife on this planet. Life never generated from nonlife in this universe. There must exist a Creator. That means there could be an absolute. All the dominoes come crashing down.

But, perhaps not all is lost. True, there must be a Creator, but that doesn't mean the Creator is an absolute-giver. Postmodern thought may not be dead. However, if the Creator is the God of the Bible, then all bets are off. But the Bible is also a row of dominoes. Tip one and they all fall. The weakest domino is Noah's Flood. The Flood never occurred. There is no geological evidence for it. Case closed! The dominoes fall. That is, unless there is another valid timeline.

Professor McCleaver argues for another potential

*timeline, the biblical timeline. However, it remains for him to prove that the biblical potential timeline is equivalent with the geological timeline. He has to prove that both potential timelines pass through the same beginning and the same ending events. But he can't succeed if, for no other reason, than that the ending event is way in the future. There is no way to prove equivalence for the future.*

At two o'clock on Thursday I enter the Student Union and proceed toward the faculty lounge. The uneasiness I felt after the Tuesday session has abated and I confidently arrive at the booth where Professor McCleaver sits.

"Professor."

"Good afternoon, Connor."

Professor McCleaver lifts his coffee mug to his lips, sips some coffee, and places the mug on the table in front of him next to his Bible and a folder of papers. The old professor studies me for a moment then begins. "Connor, today is game day. As you no doubt recall from Tuesday's meeting, you left it up to me to demonstrate that the geological and biblical potential timelines are equivalent."

Professor McCleaver holds up the diagram showing

the outlines of the three-dimensional box with two lines, one solid and the other dashed, twisting within the box to connect two events 'B' and 'E.' "The solid line is the geological timeline and the dashed line is the biblical timeline."

"Yes. I claimed that you will have to prove that both potential timelines actually pass through the same beginning and ending events."

"Connor, Event Theory makes no distinction regarding when timelines pass through an event, only that the timelines do pass through that event. Furthermore, Event Theory does not require that we know anything about other events the timelines pass through. The only requirement by Event Theory is that the geological and biblical potential timelines are equivalent, that is, both potential timelines *really do* pass through 'B' and 'E' – the same beginning event and the same ending event. Do you agree with my assessment?"

"Yes, so far."

"What remains then is to demonstrate that both timelines do describe the same beginning and the same ending events. The geological and biblical timelines pass through different and unrelated events over the course of time but, near the beginning and the ending events, the timelines should pass close enough to each other for the events to be similar. I recall that you suggested such a possibility during our last session."

"Yes, I remember saying that."

Professor McCleaver stops to sip more coffee. "The geological timeline highlights events from the beginning of the solar system and earth 4.6 billion years ago to the present. So, Connor, given your education in the field of biological sciences, what can you tell me about the beginning of earth?"

I take a few moments to recall what I learned in one of my classes about the history of Earth. "Well, from what scientists have deduced, the solar system formed within the debris cloud from the supernova of a massive star. Material that would become a proto-sun and proto-planets gradually accreted into orbital zones much as they exist today. What eventually became earth was an accretion of rocky material including radioactive elements and an enormous quantity of water."

"What was the first state of earth?"

"Heat released through gravitational compression and through fission of the radioactive material near the core heated the earth from within, and heat released from the impact of cosmic material heated the earth from without. The outcome was that earth's surface temperature was raised to the melting point. The proto-earth became a red ball of liquid rock surrounded by an enormous gaseous atmosphere. Over several hundred million years the earth cooled and the atmosphere cooled sufficiently for the water to precipitate out. This created an ocean with temperature near the boiling point covering an unstable thin crust that spasmodically formed, but was broken up by magma circulations from within the mantle and a rain of asteroids from above."

"So, the first major creation event is an earth with a global ocean?"

"Yes."

"What happened next?"

"Eventually the earth system cooled sufficiently and a thicker, stable crust formed. The process from accretion to stable crust took from one to one and a half billion years."

"So, the second major event in the evolution of earth is a stable crust. What happened next?"

"After a stable crust had formed and the oceans had cooled, primitive forms of sea life evolved in shallow seas near coastlines.

Over a period of approximately a billion years, these organisms changed the chemistry of the oceans and the atmosphere to support the evolution of different and more complex life forms. Life in the oceans continued to diversify until reaching a maximum during the so-called 'Cambrian Explosion' 600 million years ago."

"I see. The third major event in earth's history is the evolution of life in the oceans."

"Since you are keeping track of events, the fourth major event is life evolving on land around 400 million years ago."

"Then I take it that the fifth major event is the appearance of man?"

"Yes. The precursors to man appeared around three million years ago."

"Let me summarize what you have just told me about the origin of the earth and life. There are five major events in the history of earth and its life forms.

1. Water covers earth
2. Dry land appears
3. Life evolves in Oceans
4. Animals evolve on Land
5. Man appears on scene

"Do you agree?"

"Yes. In general, that is what I have been taught."

"Now, Connor, if the biblical potential timeline is equivalent with the geological potential timeline, we would expect the biblical creation narrative to be comparable with these five events, would we not?"

"Yes."

"Let's see. First, the story begins with earth covered with water. '…and the Spirit of God was moving over the surface of the waters.' Genesis 1:2; 'God made the expanse, and separated the waters which were below the expanse from the waters which were above the expanse; and it was so.' Genesis 1:7.

"Second, the dry land appears. 'Then God said, "Let the waters below the heavens be gathered into one place and let the dry land appear"; and it was so.' Genesis 1:9.

"Third, the Bible records the creation of sea creatures. 'Then God said, "Let the waters teem with swarms of living creatures..."' Genesis 1:20.

"Fourth, the Bible records the creation of living creatures on land. 'Then God said, "Let the earth bring forth living creatures after their kind: cattle and creeping things and beasts of the earth after their kind;" and it was so.' Genesis 1:24.

"And fifth, man. 'Then God said, "Let Us make man in Our image, according to Our likeness..."' Genesis 1:26."

Professor McCleaver pauses for another sip of coffee. "So how does the biblical record compare with the geological record?

| | |
|---|---|
| 1. Water covers earth | 1. Water |
| 2. Dry land appears | 2. Dry land appears |
| 3. Life evolves in Oceans | 3. Sea Creatures |
| 4. Animals evolve on Land | 4. Land Animals |
| 5. Man appears on scene | 5. Man |

"Our lists of events yield five for five! That means science and the Bible describe the same beginning.

Keep in mind that Event Theory keeps track of timelines that pass through specified events. Event Theory does not care about when those passages occur. So, Connor, what is your conclusion?"

"It seems the two potential timelines do pass through the same beginning, at least close enough to be equivalent. But what about the ending? The timelines have to pass through both events."

"Speaking of timelines, we are out of time. We will have to take up equivalence of the ending event next Tuesday. Come prepared to tell me how science understands the ending of earth."

CHAPTER 18

# SESSION SIXTEEN: THE ENDING

On Tuesday afternoon, I reflect as I approach the Student Union. *This is Professor McCleaver's big day. He gets to try, at least, to show that the geological and biblical timelines pass through the same ending event. What if he does demonstrate equivalence? What would he gain? Would he be able to answer my second objection to Noah's Flood?*

I arrive on time at the faculty lounge. Professor McCleaver is sipping from his coffee mug.

"Good afternoon, Connor."

Professor McCleaver holds up the diagram showing the outlines of the three-dimensional box with two lines, one solid and the other dashed, connecting to two common events. Pointing to 'E' he begins. "Are you ready to tell me what happens to earth in the future?"

"Yes."

"I want to remind you. Event Theory makes no distinction regarding when a timeline passes through an event, only that the timeline *does* pass through that event. The only requirement by Event Theory is that the geological and biblical potential timelines are equivalent, that is, both potential timelines *really* pass through 'B' and 'E' – the same beginning event and the same ending event. Do you agree with my assessment?"

"Yes. That is where we started last week."

"Let me summarize where we finished regarding the origin of the earth and life. There are five major events in the origin of earth and its life forms. This is how the geological and biblical timelines line up.

| | |
|---|---|
| 1. Water covers earth | 1. Water |
| 2. Dry land appears | 2. Dry Land |
| 3. Life evolves in Oceans | 3. Sea Creatures |
| 4. Animals evolve on Land | 4. Land Animals |
| 5. Man appears on scene | 5. Man |

"Our lists of events yielded five for five. Science and the Bible describe the same beginning. As I recall, you agreed with me that both potential timelines do pass through the same beginning."

"Yes."

"And what remains is to demonstrate that the two potential timelines pass through the same ending?"

"Yes."

"Are you prepared to describe what scientists tell us about the ending of earth?"

"Yes."

"Let's get started."

I begin. "According to what we know, or think we know, between four and five billion years from now the sun will exhaust its available supply of hydrogen for fusion into helium. The sun will 'nova.' This does not mean that the sun will explode as do larger and more massive stars, but rather that the sun will go through several stages as it declines from the star we see today to just another object in space.

"The temperature of the sun will rise and the diameter of the sun will expand, eventually reaching almost as far as the orbit of earth. When this happens, a number of events will occur on earth. First, anything that can burn will burn. That includes grass, trees, houses, buildings, the contents thereof, and soil of organic origin."

"So, the first event is that it gets so hot that everything combustible burns."

"Yes. Second, as the sun's surface expands toward earth, the blast of energetic particles will create an enormously powerful solar wind. The solar wind will strip away the earth's atmosphere."

"The second event is the loss of Earth's atmosphere."

"Third, the extreme heat will melt the ground. Since the remaining rocks that make up the ground are of volcanic origin, they will return to a magma state. The landscape will flow with rivers of lava."

"The third event is the melting of at least the surface layer of the earth's crust."

"Fourth, the oceans will boil away. The intense heat and loss of atmospheric pressure will convert all the water to steam, which will then be blown away by the solar wind."

"The oceans boil away."

"Yes. And fifth, darkness. Eventually the sun will

deplete its reservoir of hydrogen. When that happens, the sun will collapse on itself. The sun will shrink to a white-hot body which, if viewed in the night sky, would appear about the size of Jupiter. The sun will slowly cool, passing from a white dwarf to a brown dwarf and eventually cool to an unseen object in the darkness of space."

"So, to summarize what you have just reported, there are five events that will characterize the demise of earth as we know it.

1. Everything burns
2. Atmosphere stripped away
3. Rocks melt
4. Oceans boil away
5. Darkness

"Am I correct? And all of this will happen four to five billion years from now?"

"Yes. These five points summarize what I have been taught."

"Not a good time to be alive, is it?"

Professor McCleaver pauses to sip some coffee. I

smile as I reply. "I don't think we need to worry about that. Mankind will have vanished long before these events happen."

"How so?"

"We could destroy each other in a nuclear war. We could wear out the earth's resources and starve. Or there could be a mass-extinction event such as an asteroid impact."

Professor McCleaver pauses for more coffee. Then he questions, "What if I told you that the Bible identifies exactly the same five events as occurring at the time of the end of the earth?"

"You would have to demonstrate that to be the case."

"What if I told you that mankind will be present on earth when these events occur?"

"I would be skeptical of any claim of mankind populating earth four to five billion years from now."

"Connor, the biblical potential timeline passes through the earth-ending event far sooner than does the geological potential timeline."

"Oh, yes. I forgot about that."

"Allow me to demonstrate that the biblical potential

timeline passes through the same ending event."

Professor McCleaver sips more coffee then continues. "Anything the Bible tells us about the end is, by definition, prophecy. Whenever the Bible tells of the end, it is in reference to 'Day of Judgment' or 'Day of the Lord.' According to the ancient prophets, a number of events will occur.

"First, everything that can burn will burn. 'They will look at one another in astonishment, their faces aflame.' Isaiah 13:8. 'Therefore, a curse devours the earth and those who live in it are held guilty. Therefore, the inhabitants of the earth are burned, and few men are left.' Isaiah 24:6. 'But the present heavens and earth, by His word are being reserved for fire, kept for the Day of Judgment and destruction of ungodly men.' 2 Peter 3:7.

"Second, the atmosphere will pass away. '... and the sky will be rolled up like a scroll...' Isaiah 34.4. 'But the day of the Lord will come as a thief, in which the heavens will pass away with a roar...' 2 Peter 3:10.

"Third, the elements will melt. 'The mountains melted like wax in the presence of the Lord.' Psalms 97:5. '... the elements will be destroyed with intense heat...' 2 Peter 3:10.

"Fourth, the oceans will vanish. 'And I saw a new heaven and a new earth; for the first heaven and the first earth passed away, and there is no longer any sea.' Revelation 21:1.

"And fifth, darkness! 'No longer will you have the sun for light by day, nor for brightness will the moon give you light; but you will have the Lord for an everlasting light...' Isaiah 60:19. 'But in those days, after that tribulation, the sun will be darkened and the moon will not give its light...' Mark 13:24. 'And the city has no need of the sun or of the moon to shine upon it, for the glory of God has illuminated it, and its lamp is the Lamb.' Revelation 21:23.

"Simply put, there will not be a sun to shine and the moon will not be reflecting sunlight. Light for the earth will come from a different source."

The old professor pauses for another sip of coffee. "So, Connor, how does the biblical description of the end event compare with the description science offers?

| | |
|---|---|
| 1. Everything burns | 1. Fire |
| 2. Atmosphere stripped away | 2. Atmosphere passes away |

3. Rocks melt                3. Elements melt
4. Oceans boil away          4. No sea
5. Darkness                  5. No need for a sun

"Again, the results are five for five! Science and the Bible describe the same beginning and Science and the Bible describe the same ending. That means both potential timelines have to be equivalent."

I look on with nothing to say.

"Connor, our analyses of the geological and biblical potential timelines shows that both are equivalent, that is, both do pass through the same beginning event and the same ending event. That means both potential timelines are equally valid just like both timelines for Jon and Jim through Flatville were equivalent and equally valid.

"Let's take this up at our next meeting on Thursday. We will take a closer look at some of the implications of equivalency."

CHAPTER 19

# SESSION SEVENTEEN: IMPORTANCE OF EQUIVALENCE

I am the last to arrive at Wally's Pub on Wednesday evening. I quietly take my seat and place my order. It seems the rest of the group sense a meaning to my quietness and so sit silently, looking at me. Taking their attention as my cue, I point to Demetrius. "It was a train-wreck."

Demetrius studies me as the others turn toward him. Then he speaks in a quiet voice. "The two timelines are equivalent, aren't they?"

"Tell me again what you mean by equivalence," pleads Megan.

"It means the two timelines pass through the same beginning event and the same ending event," offers Demetrius. "In other words, if you begin from a starting event, the two timelines will take you on different paths through different but equally credible events to the same finish event."

I follow, "Last Thursday I gave Professor McCleaver five key highlights in the evolution of earth and its life forms. First, the planet was initially covered with water; second, the earth's crust formed; third, life evolved in the oceans; fourth, animal life evolved on land; and fifth, man evolved. This all took place over a period of four and a half billion years."

"And McCleaver was able to show the same five steps for the Bible?" queries Megan.

"All five steps in the same order."

"How did he pull off the ending?" queries Jason.

"He did that yesterday. I provided McCleaver with five steps for the ending of earth, when the sun goes through its nova. First, the earth heats up to a temperature hot enough so that everything that is combustible burns. Second, the atmosphere is stripped away by the solar wind; third, the intense heat melts the ground; fourth, the oceans boil away; and fifth, the sun fades away leaving darkness."

"And the Bible predicts all that?" questions Sean in astonishment.

"Five for five! Not only that, but the predictions are made in multiple places throughout the old and new testaments."

"Equivalence!" exclaims Demetrius. "That means Noah's Flood actually happened."

"On one timeline, complete with Noah and his family's being eyewitnesses."

"Let's see," follows Demetrius with his face twisted in thought. "Noah's Flood and the mass extinction event that took out the dinosaurs could have been the same event. It just occurred at different times depending on which timeline we are on."

"Maybe both timelines," follows Sean.

"Whoa!" exclaims Jason. "I can't get my brain wrapped around this. We know we can see light coming from galaxies that are ten billion light years away. How can that happen if we are on a timeline that passed through the creation event just six thousand years ago?"

"Maybe we really are on both timelines," answers Sean.

Salome, who has been quiet until now, speaks up. "All of this conversation is so far above me that I can't understand a thing of what you are saying. It seems like nonsense to me. It's like the whole argument is crazy. Do any of you know what you are talking about?"

We all stare at each other in silence. After a few moments, Demetrius announces, "Maybe we really don't know what we are talking about."

Then he turns toward me. "Connor, are you meeting with the Professor tomorrow?"

"Yes. McCleaver wants to talk about some of the implications of equivalency. Maybe I can get some information that will help Salome."

"And maybe the rest of us."

It's Thursday afternoon and I am on my way to the Student Union. Professor McCleaver was successful in demonstrating equivalence between the geological and biblical potential timelines. The potential timelines are equally valid. But what does that mean? It could mean that the events that occurred along each timeline are equally credible. That means that the Flood actually occurred, just not on the geological timeline. Professor McCleaver still has a lot to prove.

I arrive at the faculty lounge at two o'clock. Professor McCleaver is sipping from his coffee mug. The diagram showing the two potential timelines passing through the events beginning at 'B' and ending at 'E' lies in front of him.

"Welcome, Connor. Shall we begin?"

"Yes. It seems that you have demonstrated that the geological and biblical potential timelines are equivalent. But the remaining question is: So what? What does Event Theory gain us?"

"That's a good question. But to answer it we have to go back to where we began. As long as the evolutionary dominoes stood, the 4.5-billion-year geological timeline was all that was necessary for teachers to build the currently accepted postmodern belief system. There was no need to search for alternatives.

"By showing that prebiotic evolution is not possible in this universe, I tipped over the evolutionary dominoes and the intellectual foundation for postmodernism fell with them. If life cannot come into being through naturalistic processes, then we face the existence of a Creator. If we face the existence of a Creator, then we face the existence of an absolute."

"Yes, I understand all of that."

"Connor, you need to understand that a lot hangs on the domino of prebiotic evolution. Even though you now know and have accepted that the prebiotic evolution domino has been tipped over, many in the academic world will nevertheless cling to the false hope that someday a viable theory of prebiotic evolution will be discovered. That is why prebiotic evolution is still taught in your biology textbook, and that is why science popularizers still proclaim that, if water is found on a celestial body, then the presence of life cannot be far behind."

"I understand."

"With the fall of prebiotic evolution, the naturalistic geological timeline includes no life-generating events because supernatural events are disallowed. If we are to understand how living organisms were created, we will have to search along other timelines for earth, timelines that do pass through life-generating events."

"Like the biblical timeline?"

"Yes. Enter Event Theory. Event Theory expands the range of possibilities. In our previous sessions I showed that the current naturalistic geological timeline and the biblical timeline are equivalent. We agree that there could exist a possibly infinite number of potential timelines that could also satisfy the equivalence criteria."

"True. But you pointed out that the geological and biblical timelines are the only equivalent timelines we know about. How can we know of the existence of any others?

"We are going to find out. I am increasing the complexity of our search for valid timelines by retaining only those equivalent potential timelines that pass through life-creation events. This additional requirement reduces the number of candidate timelines considerably. In fact, this additional requirement eliminates the current naturalistic geological timeline from our list of candidate potential timelines. The naturalistic geological timeline only passes through the haloes of the creation events.

"In its place, there is one equivalent timeline much

like the currently accepted geological timeline except that it allows for passage through supernatural creation events. Do you know about 'old earth creation'?"

"No."

"Those who hold to 'old earth creation' claim that the Creator created at various times over the 4.6 billion years of geological history. It could be that they have it right and we need look no further than the modified geological timeline they have proposed."

"Then the biblical timeline is not necessary to solve the origin-of-life problem?"

"That could be. But then again, maybe the authors of the modified geological timeline don't have it right."

Professor McCleaver pauses for a sip of coffee. "Connor, we have demolished the foundation for postmodernism and have established that life *must* have been created. Therefore, there must exist a Creator. What is now important is this: the potential timelines that do pass through the life-creation events can tell us much about the character of the Creator and the purposes, if any, for the creation. For example, the Creator along the modified geological timeline could have established an absolute or could be an 'impersonal force' or an 'intelligent designer' with no particular purpose for the creation.

"In contrast, the biblical timeline tells us about a Creator who had a plan and is subsequently involved in intimate relationship with his creation. He rules as a King of kings and therefore can be expected to have established one or more absolutes."

I summarize. "Okay. So, what I think I hear you saying is that the geological timeline can be made to pass through creation events. The presence of the fossil record tells us what the Creator created and when over periods of hundreds of millions of years. Furthermore, the Creator may or may not have had purposes in doing so."

"Correct. But there is more. The fossil record tells us about the character of the Creator. The fossil record is a record of death over long periods of time. That means the Creator has to be comfortable with death, mass death, extinctions, bloody supremacy battles, and fang and claw predator/prey engagements."

"I think I'm getting it. The existing naturalistic geological timeline does not allow for life-creation events so we need other timelines that do. Event

Theory allows for the existence of these other timelines. The only requirements are that the timelines are equivalent and pass through life-generating events. Furthermore, these timelines can tell us much about the character of the Creator."

"Correct. Equivalence is hugely important. Equivalence disqualifies those timelines that pass through life-creation events but do not satisfy equivalence criteria. There are many religious systems and cultures that have their own creation narratives, but to my knowledge they are not equivalent! Buddhism, Islam, and even the Enuma Elish of the ancient Sumerians don't make it. None of them describe the past beginning of earth nor the future ending of earth in the detail shown by the modified geological and biblical timelines."

"Wow! Are you saying that, of all the potential timelines that pass through life-creation events, there are only two that satisfy equivalency and life-generation?"

"As far as I know. Furthermore, through equivalency, Event Theory gives both timelines equal validity. This implies that the events found on the biblical timeline are as credible as events that define the modified geological timeline."

The old professor stops for more coffee. Then, leaning back in his seat, he continues. "So, have I answered your question about what Event Theory gains us?"

"I think so. If I understand your argument, Event Theory does several things. First, instead of a single timeline, Event Theory postulates an infinite number of potential timelines passing through an infinite number of events. Second, through equivalency, Event Theory proposes many potential timelines that could explain the history of earth. Third, by retaining only those equivalent timelines that pass through life-creation events, you reduced the number of equivalent potential timelines to just two, as you see it. Fourth, by examining the two equivalent potential timelines you selected, you were able to deduce characteristics of the Creator. Fifth, by requiring equivalence, you were able to disqualify those potential timelines of other religious systems which claim to pass through creation events. And sixth, you showed through equivalency that the events along the biblical timeline are just as credible as the events that occurred along the modified geological timeline."

Professor McCleaver sips more coffee. "Connor, because of equivalence, Event Theory changes our perception of the biblical record from that of a naïve ancient myth to a credible historical narrative substantiated by eyewitness accounts. Those accounts describe a world-changing mass extinction event that occurred during the lifetime of Noah. Therefore, the Flood domino still stands!"

For a few moments I stare at Professor McCleaver with nothing to say. Then an idea comes to mind and I declare, "I still have one remaining question."

"Which is?"

"How can the geological timeline pass through the halo of life-creation events hundreds of millions of years ago if the biblical timeline passes through the actual creation only a few thousand years ago?"

"Connor, in the usual way we understand time, an event doesn't happen until we experience it. So, it would be reasonable to infer that there is some sort of contradiction if the creation event occurred six thousand years ago yet the haloes of the same events occurred hundreds of millions of years ago. However, in Event Theory, the existence times for events are independent of human observation. That the biblical timeline intersected with the creation events about six thousand years ago does not mean that the creation events first existed six thousand years ago. The creation events may have been present in event space for billions of years."

I look at the old professor with confusion. Noticing my facial expression, he takes a deep breath and exhales, directing his breath upward to flutter the curls in his white hair. "Okay," he mutters. "Look at your question from the perspective of time. The naturalistic geological timeline passed through the haloes of the creation events hundreds of millions of years ago. The geological timeline modified for supernatural events passed through the creation events hundreds of millions of years ago also, did it not?"

"Oh, yes. I guess it did. I didn't think of that."

"In Event Theory, an event and its halo can exist for long periods of time before any timeline passes through it. The life-creation events could have been in the mind of the Creator perhaps before the foundation of the world."

The Professor sips more coffee. "I will see you at our next meeting on Tuesday."

CHAPTER 20

# SESSION EIGHTEEN: A COMMON EVENT

On Tuesday I arrive at the Student Union faculty lounge just after two. Professor McCleaver sits with his coffee mug and papers spread before him just like last Thursday.

"Welcome, Connor. Any questions related to our last session?"

"All of the stuff we discussed seems like an alternate reality."

"Yes. But which alternate reality? Is the biblical record an alternate reality or is the geological record an alternate reality? Maybe both. And, for that matter, what about the future? Which potential timeline are we really on? Or are we on both potential timelines?"

Professor McCleaver pauses to sip some coffee. "Connor, what makes understanding Event Theory all the more difficult is that, other than at the events 'B' and 'E,' the events on the geological and biblical timelines, though equally credible, are not related. That means, if one exclusively follows the geological timeline, he will not have a framework with which to comprehend events on the biblical timeline and vice versa."

"Are there any places in history other than the beginning and ending events that the two timelines have in common?"

Professor McCleaver draws back in his seat while lifting his hand to his chin. His brow furrows. "Perhaps there is another event the timelines hold in common. That is the formation of the Jordan Rift Valley.

"Geological scientists have postulated that the Jordan Rift Valley began forming ten to twenty million years ago when the Arabian Plate separated from Africa. Then about one million years later, the land between the Mediterranean and the Jordan Rift Valley rose so that sea water stopped flooding the area. Once the intrusions of sea water were cut off, the mass of water contained in the flooded valley gradually evaporated to levels near those observed today."

The old professor sips more coffee. Then he leans forward while looking directly at me. "The biblical timeline encountered the Jordan Valley event differently. The biblical patriarch Abraham and his nephew Lot traveled from the city of Ur in the Sumerian Empire, which was located in what is today Iraq, southward to the land of Canaan, which today is Palestine. They continued into Egypt then turned back to Canaan, where Abraham spent the rest of his life herding sheep and cattle over the surrounding hills.

"Abraham's geography of the Jordan Valley can be inferred from what the Bible records and what it doesn't. He referred to the Jordan valley as the 'Valley of Siddim' – translated as a broad flat valley. Abraham described the Jordan Valley as supporting a number of city states, each with its own king, who were at times at war with each other.

"As their flocks and herds multiplied, disputes arose over grazing lands. Abraham and Lot discovered that they would have to go their separate ways. Abraham gave Lot first choice. Given that option, Lot decided to take the best land for himself. He saw that the Jordan valley was well-watered and lush green with vegetation, so he moved his herds to the valley while Abraham remained in the hill country."

I interrupt. "That doesn't describe the Jordan Valley we see today."

"No, it doesn't. Because, on the biblical timeline, the Jordan Valley event had not yet happened. But there's more. Abraham's record makes no mention - not one word by any name - of the Sea of Galilee. Abraham's record makes no mention of the Dead Sea. There is only a parenthetical reference to the Dead Sea inserted into Abraham's text by a later redactor. Furthermore, Abraham's description of the Jordan Valley that Lot chose, 'well watered everywhere, like the garden of the Lord, like the land of Egypt as you go to Zoar,' carries with it the caveat '...this was before the Lord destroyed Sodom and Gomorrah.' This tells us that an event was coming that would, at the very least, change the ecology of the Valley.

"In the meantime, however, Abraham's geography of the Valley of Siddim is that of a wide, flat, well-watered lush valley everywhere that harbored a number of city states with significant human population. Most importantly, the Valley of Siddim harbored no bodies of water of nameable size."

The professor pauses for another sip of coffee. "Now let's take a look at Lot's actions. Abraham recorded that Lot moved his tents as far as Sodom. Abraham also recorded that Lot surveyed and chose 'all of the valley' of the Jordan for himself. The word that has been translated 'valley' literally means 'circle.' This has led some commentators to assume that 'circle' referred to a local area surrounding Sodom and Gomorrah.

"However, a different reading holds that 'circle' is not the name for a local area, especially since no definable circular areas existed, but rather for the action of viewing the entire valley, first by looking to the north, then around to the northeast, then east, then southeast, then south. Thus, a person viewing the full length of the Jordan Valley would turn his head one-hundred and eighty degrees or in a half-circle to completely view the valley. This second interpretation makes the most sense considering that Lot would likely not have been interested in the valley if only the area around Sodom and Gomorrah was lush green and well-watered."

I interrupt to summarize. "So, Abraham's description of the Jordan Valley before the destruction of Sodom and Gomorrah argues that the ecology of the valley was different from what it is today and that the geography of the valley was different also, because the valley was not as deep as it is today."

"Yes. Abraham went on to describe the Jordan Valley event. He saw smoke along the full length of the valley rising like 'smoke from a furnace.' In those days the furnace was used for smelting and was the hottest fire men of his time had produced. Smoke from a furnace rose in tight boiling billows. Abraham was describing a volcanic eruption, something like Mount Saint Helens, along the full length of the valley. Abraham witnessed the event as having 'destroyed *all* of the cities of the valley, *all* of the valley, *all* of the inhabitants of the valley, and having burned up *every* green thing.'"

Professor McCleaver sips more coffee. Then he summarizes. "What Abraham described was a major eruption along the Great Rift Valley, an eruption that changed all features of the valley. This means that both the geological and biblical potential timelines passed through the Jordan Valley event but not at the same time nor in the same manner. The geological timeline intersected the Jordan Valley event during a period of between five and twenty-five million years ago. The biblical timeline intersected the Jordan Valley event during the lifetime of Abraham."

He watches me as I try to absorb his descriptions of the Jordan Valley event. Then he smiles. "Connor, this is a lot of information, and once you have had some time to think it over, you will undoubtedly come up with more questions. Let's continue on Thursday."

As I depart the faculty lounge, I look forward to tomorrow evening at Wally's Pub. I have a lot to think over.

"So, what happened?" begins Jason as I take my seat at Wally's Pub.

"I conceded that Professor McCleaver had proven equivalence between the geological and biblical timelines. My question was 'So what? What does Event Theory gain us?' His answer was that Event Theory opens up other potential timelines through which we can interpret reality."

"What can we know through other timelines that we don't already know with the timeline we have?" queries Megan.

"McCleaver reminded me that he had disproven prebiotic evolution. Life never evolved from nonlife on this planet nor in this universe. Then he used this conclusion to argue that the geological timeline does not pass through life-generating events."

"Wait a minute," protests Sean. "We have found meteorites with amino acids within them. There has to be life somewhere out there."

"Simple amino acids don't add up to anything as complex as life," counters Demetrius.

"Then why are we going to Mars?" asks Megan.

Demetrius replies. "I have pondered the same question. Even if we find life on Mars, we will be no closer to answering the question of how life originated. Thanks to Professor McCleaver we will only learn that life was created elsewhere in the universe. In his words, the geological timeline does not pass through life-creating events. It passes through the haloes of life-creating events."

"What do you mean by 'haloes'?" queries Salome.

"Yeah," adds Jason, "and doesn't the fossil record mean anything?"

Demetrius replies, "A halo is an aftermath of an event but not the event itself."

I follow. "The geological timeline is a naturalistic construct so it cannot pass through supernatural events. Since naturalistic prebiotic evolution of life is not possible, all we are left with are supernatural creation events. Apart from a Creator, we will never discover how life came into existence. If we accept this, we have to find another timeline along which supernatural life-generating events are possible."

"How many supernatural timelines are there?" questions Megan.

"According to Event Theory there could be millions," follows Demetrius.

"True," I reply. "But McCleaver is interested in only two."

"I guess the biblical timeline is one of those. What

would be the other timeline?" questions Megan.

"The current geological timeline modified to flow through supernatural events. Ever hear about 'old-earth creation'?"

"No."

"A lot of people hold these views. But McCleaver objects because a divinized geological timeline constrains the Creator to create only certain organisms over periods of hundreds of millions of years. Furthermore, the god of the geological timeline wouldn't have to have purpose in creation so there wouldn't necessarily have to be any absolutes. The God of the Bible is personal, as Megan discovered, and therefore would be more likely to have set up absolutes, at least according to the professor."

Sean queries, "Why is McCleaver interested in only two potential timelines? It seems there could be many timelines that satisfy his equivalence criteria."

"True. But so far, the professor has found only two potential timelines that satisfy equivalence and that pass through life-generating events. Other religions and cultures have creation narratives but, according to the professor, the timelines for these religions are not equivalent."

"Hmmm," muses Sean. "Several weeks ago, it seemed to me that McCleaver was pushing Connor toward the God of the Bible for no good reason. Salome noted that gods of other religions also could put forth absolutes."

"I remember saying that," interjects Salome. "And Connor supported me. He said that his religion professors claimed that all religions are basically the same so it doesn't matter which religion and which god one chooses."

"But it does matter," continues Sean. "According to McCleaver's Event Theory, the potential timelines for all of these religions are not equivalent. They are automatically disqualified as Connor just pointed out."

After moment of silence Jason changes the subject, "Anything else McCleaver presented?"

"Yes. McCleaver reiterated that the two timelines should be similar at the beginning and ending events but elsewhere may not have much correlation. However, he pointed out an event that may have been common to the two timelines - the origin of the Jordan Rift Valley. Without going into details, suffice it to say that, on the geological timeline, the valley gradually formed from five to twenty million years ago. On the biblical timeline, the valley formed over several days during the life of Abraham."

"I read in my Bible about Abraham!" exclaims Megan. "I recall that God talked with him a lot, but I don't remember anything about the formation of the Rift Valley."

"That could be because we don't have an intellectual framework for understanding the Bible," offers Demetrius. Then, looking at me he asks, "Connor, what are you and the professor going to discuss tomorrow?"

"I'm not sure. He left it up to me to ask questions."

"I have a question."

"Shoot."

"It seems to me that Professor McCleaver is pushing the biblical timeline above all other potential timelines that could satisfy the constraints of Event Theory. If we are faced with the God of the Bible as the Creator, we need to know what kind of god he is. If the fossil record is just a 'halo' of biblical creation, then I want to know why there were dinosaurs."

"You mean why a Creator would create dinosaurs?" queries Sean.

"Yes!" follows Demetrius. "What kind of Creator would create the flesh-tearing monsters we see in the fossil record? The fossil record tells us something about the character of God!"

"Not the character of the God I read about in the Bible," offers Megan. "At least not in what I've read so far."

"Ahhh! An inconsistency!" exclaims Sean. "Good point, Demetrius. The geological timeline passes through the haloes of the creation events. There are dinosaurs in the haloes. That means dinosaurs were created."

"So, Connor," summarizes Jason, "one question to ask is this: Since the geological timeline passes through the haloes of creation, what does the fossil record tell us about the God of the Bible, if the God of the Bible is actually the Creator?"

CHAPTER 21

# SESSION NINETEEN: A NEW EVOLUTION

After departing from my friends on Wednesday, I have time to ponder Jason's question. *Okay. Prebiotic evolution never happened. So, we have to have a Creator. Hmmm. What if postbiotic or Darwinian evolution never happened either? Or if Darwinian evolution happened, did it occur on a scale much smaller than we have been led to believe? That means everything we see in the fossil record was created. After all, organisms in the fossil record always appear fully formed and functional.*

*But what kind of Creator? The fossil record is a record of death, sometimes on a massive scale. The fossil record is a record of monsters, beasts designed for gnashing and dashing. But the fossil record is the 'halo' of creation events. That means the creation of dinosaurs occurred on some other timeline. What then does that tell me about the Creator? It tells me that the God of the Bible is out! That leaves the god of the modified geological timeline, possibly a god that did not set up absolutes. Could it be that postmodernism is still a viable philosophical foundation?*

On Thursday I arrive at the Student Union faculty lounge at the agreed-upon time. Professor McCleaver, prepared as usual, waits for me.

"Welcome, Connor."

"Professor."

"Any questions regarding our last session?"

"Yes. Why did God create the dinosaurs?"

"What makes you think God created the dinosaurs?"

"Well, if naturalistic evolution is not the mechanism for the rise of the dinosaurs, then that leaves a Creator as the means."

"Whoa! Why do you say that naturalistic evolution did not lead to the dinosaurs?"

"Well, you showed that prebiotic evolution never happened, so we have to have a Creator. Once you have introduced a Creator of life from nonlife, the Creator could also have created the organisms that appear in the fossil record, including the dinosaurs just as you claimed for the old earth creation timeline. It seems to me that naturalistic evolution is no longer required to get the dinosaurs. After all, organisms always appear fully functional in the fossil record."

Professor McCleaver leans back in his seat and draws his left hand to his chin. All the while he stares at me. After a few seconds, he leans forward and reminisces. "Connor, when I started my career in biology, we frequently spoke of 'missing links,' intermediate life forms that would bridge gaps between species found in the fossil record. We expected that the intermediate stages of evolution would eventually be discovered. After fifty years of searching, the gaps remain. We now view the fossil record as practically complete. As you point out, new organisms always appear fully developed.

"As geneticists explored the extreme complexity of living organisms, we turned our search toward 'macro-mutations.' Just a few key mutations could change one fully developed life form into another fully developed life form, so we thought. However, after three decades of tinkering with genes, no natural pathways to macro-mutations have turned up. At the end of my career, I gave up. I now view Darwin's theory as an elegant theory that explains variations within species, but the theory lacks sufficient explanatory power to account for the emergence of new species.

"But be advised that the scientific community has yet to concede that naturalistic evolution cannot lead to the emergence of the dinosaurs."

McCleaver visibly relaxes. He sips some coffee and ponders. "Hmmm. What kind of Creator would create flesh-tearing monsters like dinosaurs? This is a great question because it goes to the character of the Creator. However, answering your question takes us into alternate reality. Are you willing to go there?"

"Well, since you have brought me into Event Theory, it seems to me that we are already in alternate reality."

"Okay. Let's proceed."

Professor McCleaver pauses to sip more coffee then continues. "If indeed the modified geological timeline passes through creation events, then the

Creator created life incrementally over a period of about three billion years. Yes, the dinosaurs would be a part of the eons of creation.

"Now let's look at the biblical timeline. Ironically, to understand events that occurred along the biblical timeline, we have to understand evolution. How do you define evolution, Connor?"

"Well, from a general perspective, evolution can be defined as gradual development from simple to complex."

"Yes, one can think of the evolution of certain forms of art or of music. But to be more specific, how does the definition apply to biology?"

"Most of my teachers speak of evolution as any net directional change or any cumulative change in the characteristics of organisms or populations over many generations."

"What determines the 'characteristics' of organisms?"

"Genetics."

"Then evolution may be regarded as any net directional change or any cumulative change in the genetics of organisms or populations over many generations?"

"Yes. I would think so."

"What causes genetic change?"

"Mutations."

"Then the mechanism of evolution would be?"

"Mutation, reproduction, and natural selection as Darwin proposed."

"I suggest that mutation is just one of several sources for genetic change. Might I redefine the mechanism of evolution as 'genetic change, reproduction, and natural selection'?"

"Sure, I guess. What other sources for genetic change are there?"

"By replacing 'mutation' with 'genetic change' I am making my definition for evolution broader than the neo-Darwinian definition. So, we need to explore possibilities for genetic change other than mutations."

After the professor pauses to sip more coffee, he proceeds. "Let's start with mutations. There could be many causes for random mutations. Let's class them as 'random mutations caused by sources from outside of organisms' and 'random mutations caused by sources from within organisms.' Are you okay with these two categories?"

"Sure."

"Can you give me some examples?"

"Yes. For sources from outside of organisms, biologists think that high-energy radiation from the sun, cosmic rays, or fission of nuclear material can cause mutations. For sources from inside of organisms, biologists think small coding errors can lead to genetic mutations. But you are claiming the existence of non-mutational sources for genetic change, aren't you?"

"I am. Let's explore the possibilities. Suppose some organisms possess genetic 'switches' which, when given some kind of external stimulus, genetically alter progeny to adapt to the stimulus. Would you consider the possibility of the existence of such systems within some organisms?"

"I guess that would be possible. Actually, one of my professors described aphids in that way. Aphids are typically weak fliers and don't fly very high. But for some reason, perhaps from a stimulus involving declining or aging food sources, a new generation of aphids hatches, and these aphids are adapted for high-level, longrange flight. Once these aphids fly to distant food sources and lay their eggs, their progeny return to the weak flier stage. No net evolution has occurred; they still remain aphids. But the idea of genetic switches might not be farfetched."

"Good. Let's call this mechanism for genetic change 'latent capacity within the organism for genetic change.'"

Professor McCleaver pauses to sip more coffee. "I can think of three sources for genetic change external to the organism. Let's consider the possibility of the existence within the biosphere of organisms that possess the ability to modify the genetics of other organisms to some advantage."

"Such as?"

"Man has been involved in animal and plant breeding for centuries. More recently, man has experimented in direct gene modification. For example, scientists have produced frost resistant plants and mosquitoes that don't transmit deadly diseases."

Professor McCleaver smiles as he sips some coffee. Then he continues. "Since manipulation within other organisms is involved, let's call this mechanism 'genetic manipulation of organisms by other organisms.'"

"Hmmm, I take it that your other two mechanisms for genetic change involve manipulation also?"

"They do. Some traditions hold that the world is populated with non-material beings of great intelligence and power. These beings could possess the ability to modify the genetics of other living organisms."

"Hmmm. I gather the beings you propose operate in this physical universe but are not part of the biosphere."

"Correct. Let's call it 'genetic manipulation of organisms by nonphysical beings within the world.'

Finally, we can imagine that outside of the universe of space and time there could exist one or more non-material beings of great intelligence and power. These beings could possess the ability to modify the genetics of living organisms. This would be, let's say, 'genetic manipulation of organisms by nonphysical beings beyond the world.'

"Allow me to summarize the six mechanisms for evolution.

1. Random mutation with source external to the organism;
2. Random mutation with source internal to the organism;
3. Latent capacity for genetic change within the organism;
4. Genetic manipulation of organisms by other organisms;
5. Genetic manipulation of organisms by nonphysical beings within the world;
6. Genetic manipulation of organisms by nonphysical beings beyond the world."

Professor McCleaver pauses and looks directly at me. "Welcome to a larger world. Darwin could only see natural processes leading to genetic change. I take it the possibilities for genetic change through manipulation by non-material beings were not discussed in your biology classes."

"No!"

"Or religion classes?"

"No."

"There is not enough time to begin now. Let's take it up next Tuesday."

CHAPTER 22

# SESSION TWENTY: ORIGIN OF DINOSAURS

On Tuesday I arrive at the Student Union faculty lounge at two o'clock. Professor McCleaver is waiting for me.

"Welcome, Connor."

"Professor."

"Do you remember the question that started our last session?"

"Yes. Why did God create the dinosaurs?"

"And my answer?"

"What makes you think God created the dinosaurs?"

"As I recall, I proposed that there is more to evolution than Darwin imagined. Instead of the neo-Darwinian mechanism for evolution - mutation, reproduction, and natural selection - I defined the mechanism for evolution as 'genetic change, reproduction, and natural selection.' That opened the door for additional explanations for genetic change."

"Yes, I remember."

"We found six possible mechanisms for evolution. Four of these mechanisms involved manipulation of genetics, two of which are non-natural in cause."

"Yes."

"Then let's continue. Recall that the six mechanisms we proposed for evolution are:

1. Random mutation with source external to the organism;
2. Random mutation with source internal to the organism;
3. Latent capacity for genetic change within the organism;
4. Genetic manipulation of organisms by other organisms;
5. Genetic manipulation of organisms by nonphysical beings within the world;

6. Genetic manipulation of organisms by nonphysical beings beyond the world."

"Yes, I remember."

Professor McCleaver sips from his coffee mug. "Now let's think along the biblical timeline. Because the biblical timeline is not constrained to pass through naturalistic events only, any or all of the above mechanisms for evolution could have been operating at various times during biblical history. However, to get a perspective on the most likely evolutionary mechanism for the emergence of carnivorous dinosaurs, we will have to return to the domino of the Flood."

I stare at the old professor with an expression of surprise.

Professor McCleaver lifts his coffee mug to his mouth and takes a number of sips as he prepares himself for a long session. He opens his Bible to Genesis and begins. "Connor, near the end of the first document of Genesis, God surveyed all that he had made and declared that it 'was very good.' Yet, in Noah's document, God said, 'I will blot out man whom I have created from the face of the land, from man to animals to creeping things and to birds of the sky...' "

McCleaver pauses, lays his Bible on the table, and looks directly at me. "Connor, between these two passages something bad happened."

He picks up his Bible again and thumbs a few pages forward. "A clue as to what happened is given in the document written by the 'Sons of Noah.' Noah is understood to have been told by God that, 'The end of all flesh has come before Me; for the earth is filled with violence because of them; and behold, I am about to destroy them with the earth.'

"Connor, according to the prophets whose writings are scattered elsewhere in the Bible, war broke out in heaven not long after the creation. The rebellion by some of the spiritual beings was put down and the instigators were banished from the spiritual realm. They made their way into the physical realm and, as a consequence, Earth and the human and animal worlds are casualties of their invasion."

"I remember reading about Adam and Eve and the forbidden fruit."

"Yes, the Fall is described in Adam's document.

It is the single most important event that occurred between the Creation and the Flood in the biblical narrative. The rule of earth was transferred from God through Adam to the leader of the rebel cabal. As defeated rebels, they would hardly be expected to be friendly to life forms that had been created according to God's plan. Specifically, they would not be friendly to man, the being whom the Bible describes as being created in the image of God."

Professor McCleaver sips more coffee and continues. "We have to consider that some of the exiled spiritual beings had the knowledge and the power to manipulate the genetics of living organisms."

"That would be the fifth mechanism for genetic change," I reply.

"Yes. The primary agent for evolutionary change during this era was likely genetic manipulation of organisms by nonphysical beings within the world. The outcome was a perversion of the human and animal world - the creation that God originally saw as 'very good.' The rebel beings used their power and intelligence to twist and torture existing life forms that God created into creatures of violence. Genetics were manipulated to produce ugly, vicious, and twisted monsters, many of which populate the fossil record we see today."

"You are suggesting that it was these rebel spiritual beings who corrupted existing organisms and that corruption eventually led to the rise of the dinosaurs?" Professor McCleaver pauses to sip some coffee. "Not quite. God created the vegetarian dinosaurs. The rebel spiritual beings twisted these into the vicious flesh-tearing monsters we often associate with the word 'dinosaur.'"

"Okay, regarding my original question, 'Did God create the bad dinosaurs?' I guess the Bible's answer is 'No!'"

"The good news is that the Bible tells that some powerful spiritual beings were removed from the world sometime in the past, possibly during the Flood of Noah. This implies that the sources for genetic change through nonmaterial beings would have been greatly diminished or eliminated."

"Hmmm, according to the Bible, is that why we only see the monsters in the fossil record, but not today?"

"Yes. Evolution is now driven by several causes, including latent capacity for genetic change within organisms, genetic manipulation of organisms by other organisms, and Darwinian evolution (random mutation both internal and external to the organism.) Regarding random mutations, we make a big mistake if we assume that mutations are the *only* mechanisms for evolution. I suggest you spend some time thinking through what we have discussed. You will undoubtedly come up with a new set of questions for our next meeting. See you Thursday."

CHAPTER 23

# SESSION TWENTY-ONE: THE BABEL QUESTION

Demetrius is the last to arrive at Wally's Pub on Wednesday evening. However, he wastes little time in starting conversation. As he takes his seat, he calls across the table to me, "So, Connor, did God create the nasty dinosaurs?"

"No, he did not."

"Then who did?"

"Invaders from outer space, according to Professor McCleaver."

"What do you mean?" queries Salome.

"Spiritual beings. According to McCleaver's view of the biblical timeline, war broke out in heaven with many spiritual beings rebelling against God. The rebellion was put down and the instigators banished from heaven. They made their way to Earth as a malevolent invading force. Earth and all life on it are casualties of that invasion."

Demetrius' facial expression stops me. He stares at me with widening eyes and his jaw slowly drops. "Holy cow!" he exclaims. "That explains a lot!"

"Try explaining some of that to me," appeals Megan.

"Spiritual beings came in and corrupted everything."

I offer. "According to McCleaver, some of the spiritual beings had power to corrupt genetics..."

"...and so twisted existing living things into evil things like some of the dinosaurs," interrupts Demetrius.

"That's what Professor McCleaver believes," I conclude.

"And that takes us from God's seeing a creation that was 'very good' to a creation that he was 'sorry he made,'" follows Megan. "At least that's how I read it from my Bible."

"So, God sent the Flood, a mass-extinction event,

to wipe it all out!" exclaims Demetrius.

"Yes," I reply, "McCleaver claims that the only record of the physical event was from the sons of Noah. However, he also claims that elsewhere in the Bible it is recorded that some of the most powerful rebel beings were taken out, possibly during the Flood event."

"They drowned?" questions Salome.

"Probably from some form of supernatural warfare," offers Demetrius.

Demetrius' brow furrows from deep thought. He concludes, "So that is the biblical story. God creates a perfect world, a utopia with no pain or suffering, which is the world that the first man and woman live in. Then some of his spiritual beings rebel and the outcome is that they invade Earth as some alien spiritual force. They instigate the fall of Adam and Eve and take over the world using their powers to corrupt everything God had made..."

"And we get the nasty dinosaurs," interrupts Sean.

"... so, God sends the Flood event to destroy a world that was no longer the world he had created but a world that had been twisted into something unspeakably evil," continues Demetrius.

"More than that," follows Jason.

"What do you mean?" questions Demetrius.

"My mother is a Christian but my father is an atheist. He says he became an atheist because he could not believe in a God who created a world filled with evil and suffering. But if you have gotten it right, evil and suffering did not originate with God. And furthermore, if the biblical story of the Flood is right, the world we live in today is not the world God created. It is the rubble of the world God created."

"Well, then," offers Sean. "God didn't create the nasty dinosaurs. Are there any other questions Connor can ask McCleaver?"

I reply, "Hmmm. Megan has been reading the Bible. Megan, have you read anything questionable?"

Megan smiles. "Well, after the Flood, Noah got drunk and cursed one of his grandsons."

We all laugh. We laugh so loud that we disturb those sitting at nearby tables.

"Incredible!" exclaims Demetrius. "Incredibly true!"

"What do you mean?" queries Megan.

"Can't you see it!" exclaims Demetrius while laughing. "Noah spent 100 years building a barge, watched as the waters washed away his city and drowned his neighbors and friends, was seasick an uncountable number of times, spent more than half a year in semi-solitary confinement with the screeching, mooing, cawing, growling, honking, howling, roaring, and chirping of an uncountable number of animals to finally reach a brave new world – a monstrous mud hole with no green thing!"

Now gesturing wildly, Demetrius inquires. "What would you do if you were Noah? I know what I would do. I would go down to the local liquor store, buy a bottle of vodka, and fry my brains!"

"Except there weren't any taverns," counsels Megan. "Noah planted a vineyard."

"That's why the story is true!" exclaims Demetrius. "Planting a vineyard is the only recourse Noah had. Think of it! He had to wait until the soils and climate became stable enough to plant grape vines. It takes two to three years for the vines to produce grapes and an additional three to four years to get vintage grapes. Then another year or two for the grape juice to ferment into wine. So, it could have been ten to fifteen years after the flood that Noah walked into his tent with a case of his best wine, fried every brain cell in his head, and when he regained some form of consciousness, cursed the wrong person. Now isn't that real life?"

"He got drunk and fell down naked in his tent," corrects Megan.

"Wait a minute!" exclaims Jason. "Demetrius, I learned some of this stuff when my mother took me to church. How did you come to know these things? You're not a Christian; you haven't been to church!"

Demetrius blushes and sits silently as the rest of us stare at him. Finally, realizing that he is not going to escape, he confesses. "Remember when Connor told us about Event Theory and I had the 'aha' moment that all of history could be fit into an event diagram?"

The rest of us nod slowly.

"Remember when I said that the Bible had been black-listed from my high school library?"

The rest of us nod again.

"When Connor reported on how Professor McCleaver had demolished postmodernism, I realized that I had been lied to for many years. That's when I went out and bought a Bible. I decided to strike out on my own, and the place to start was with the book that educators had determined I should not read."

We stare at Demetrius in silence. Then, with a delightfully chipper voice, Megan proclaims. "Wow! How far have you gotten? Have you read about Abraham?"

"I'm currently in Leviticus. Yes, I have read well past Abraham."

"Anything interesting?" queries Sean.

"God is giving people his law. If people follow his rules, all will be well with everybody."

"Law given by a god implies absolutes, doesn't it?" offers Jason.

"Sure does," I reply. "Demetrius, it looks like you have found McCleaver's 'perfect cereal.'"

"Demetrius, what's the strangest thing you have read?" inquires Megan.

"There is a lot of supernatural stuff. Strangest thing? Hmmm. I think that would have to be the confusion of languages at Babel. That was way back in Genesis before Abraham."

"I remember reading about it," returns Megan.

"But it didn't make any sense, so I moved on and forgot about it."

"Hmmm," ponders Jason. "Maybe we have a question for Connor to ask McCleaver."

"Yes!" answers Demetrius enthusiastically. "Connor. Why don't you ask the professor to explain the meaning of Babel? After all, if one is going to read this stuff, it's best to make sense of what one reads."

"Okay," I reply. "But, if we are going to spend more time finding questions that we want to ask Professor McCleaver about the Bible, I think those of us who haven't bought Bibles should get one. That way we will all be on the same page."

On Thursday I arrive at the Student Union faculty lounge. Professor McCleaver is waiting for me.

"Welcome, Connor."

"Professor."

"Have you come up with a new set of questions?"

"Yes. It seems like I am faced with a choice between either a 'divinized' naturalistic geological timeline for which unexplainable causes are replaced with 'God did it' or the biblical timeline, which passes through some supernatural events that defy reason. Since I am now faced with accepting the biblical timeline, I would like to know what some of the events mean, for example the confusion of languages at Babel."

Professor McCleaver rests his chin on his right hand. "Hmmm. You have picked a tough one. The Babel event is a major part of the biblical narrative but the Bible doesn't explain why the event occurred, only that it did. So, one must rely on extra-biblical sources, which may be speculative, or on his own intuition to help fill in the gaps."

The old professor takes a sip of coffee and picks up his Bible from the bench beside him. "Hmmm. The confusion-of-languages story is found in Genesis Chapter Eleven."

He thumbs through the book and summarizes the parts as he reads. "They start with the same language; they commence to build a city; to build a tower; hmmm, strange wording here; God comes down to see the project and disapproves; God confuses their language; hmmm, that essentially makes them all strangers; they run away from each other and there is no one left to finish the project."

McCleaver puts down his Bible and stares at me. "Connor, what parts of this story do you question?"

"The whole story seems farfetched to me. However, on second thought, in all of my classes on evolution, no one has explained the emergence of languages."

"I have three questions," replies the professor. "The first is the definition of 'they' in verse two, the second is the strange wording of verse four, and the third is God's disapproval of the project."

McCleaver pauses to sip some coffee from his mug. "My first question is, 'how many people make up the "they" in verse two?' We know that eight people, Noah and his wife and Noah's three sons and their wives, disembarked the ark. We need to find out how many generations passed until they built the city."

After picking up his Bible and thumbing through several pages while mumbling to himself, Professor McCleaver looks up at me and proclaims, "Ah, I found it. Chapter Ten, verse nine, Nimrod; verse ten, beginning of his kingdom was Babel, hmmm, in the land of Shinar. Now let's see; Nimrod was the son of

Cush; hmmm, and Cush was the son of Ham, one of Noah's three sons. Ham, Cush, and Nimrod; three generations. Well, almost three generations."

I look on as McCleaver rummages through a folder. He produces his time-age diagram and a spread-sheet. Pointing to the spread-sheet he explains, "Connor, this is the spread-sheet I used to create the time-age diagram."

Mumbling to himself as he thumbs down the spread-sheet, he looks up again. "Let's assume that the descendents of Ham lived as long as the descendents of Shem. Shem lived six hundred years. Hmmm, his son, Arpachshad, lived four-hundred thirty-eight years. Let's assume that Ham lived as long as Shem and that Cush lived as long as Arpachshad. Shem's grandson, Selah, lived four-hundred thirty-three years. Assume Nimrod lived to the same age."

McCleaver studies his time-age diagram then proclaims. "According to my time-age diagram, Shelah outlived Abraham. If Nimrod lived as long as Shelah, he also was alive during the lifetime of Abraham. Depending on when Nimrod started his project, he could have had access to as many as nine generations of humankind to do the work. So, depending on the birth rates, Nimrod could have had access to tens of thousands of people to build his empire."

McCleaver pauses to sip more coffee. "Question two; the strange wording in verse four. Hmmm, 'a tower that will reach into heaven.' Hmmm, the plain of Shinar. Connor, the passage tells us that, after the Flood, humanity found its way to a flat plain and settled there. That there were no high places is important to the biblical narrative. High places were where men went to worship their gods. I suggest that the tower at Babel was not intended as a high-rise office building but as a high place to sacrifice to spiritual beings other than the one true God."

"So that is why God confused their languages?" I inquire.

"Yes. And that answers my question three. God was not offended that they were building a tall structure. Goodness! Look at buildings today. God was offended because men were turning away from him to worship false gods."

The professor raises his mug to his lips and swallows more coffee.

"Connor, God's confusing the languages at Babel did not stop men from worshiping false gods, but the act did buy him time to implement a new plan to build a holy nation through one man."

"Abraham?"

"Yes. And through Abraham's descendents, God would enter the human world as a man."

"Jesus?"

"Correct. And through Jesus, God reconciled mankind to himself. That means that the God of the Bible has been, is, and will be interested in and active with the affairs of men. And that means we will always have an absolute."

Professor McCleaver leans back in his seat and looks at me. I reply, "I've been discussing our sessions with a group of friends. We are starting a Bible study on Wednesday evening at Wally's Pub."

McCleaver smiles broadly. "Good. I believe I have brought you to where you need to be. Now you are ready for the last question, the answer to which drives the final nail into the coffin of postmodernism. It is also the reason why I have been favoring the biblical potential timeline when possible, during our discussions. It is also the primary reason why your religion professors spend time disparaging Christianity."

The old professor's smile fades. "Unfortunately, we are out of time today. Since your group is beginning to study the Bible, I would like to stretch our sessions out to once a week. Let's meet again next Thursday. In the meantime, I will give all of you an assignment. You can relay my assignment to your friends when you meet with them tomorrow. Begin your Bible study with the New Testament and read all of the four gospels - Matthew, Mark, Luke, and John. Then discuss your readings when you gather again. When you return next Thursday be prepared to discuss what you have found."

CHAPTER 24

# SESSION TWENTY-TWO: FINAL QUESTION

Late Wednesday afternoon I arrive at Wally's Pub with my backpack of books, Bible included. Demetrius, Sean, and Jason have already secured a table in a corner - thus making our session semi-private. Megan and Salome arrive a few minutes later. After we place our orders, Sean opens with a question. "Connor, what did Professor McCleaver have to say about the Tower of Babel?"

"It's an interesting story. People of that time preferred to worship their gods on high places like hills or mountains. The Bible relates that the people, perhaps tens of thousands of people according to McCleaver, migrated to a low flat plain where there were no high places…"

"How did McCleaver determine that there were that many people?"

"Could have been more. He assumed that, for each generation, the descendants of Ham lived as long as the descendents of Shem. Having made that assumption, Professor McCleaver could use Terah's geneology to estimate how long Nimrod lived. It turns out that Nimrod was alive during Abraham's lifetime. That means that Nimrod could have had nine generations of humans to work with. So, the actual number of people who populated Nimrod's empire depended on how old he was when he started it."

I pause for a sip of beer. "Also, it is likely families were very large."

"Seems to me that is an ambitious production," offers Salome.

"I suspect that building large families was more central to the culture back then than it is today."

"Does that mean women were more central to the culture back then than they are today?" queries Demetrius with a smile.

Both Megan and Salome scowl at Demetrius. "I

felt that jab," grumbles Megan.

"Maybe that explains why women today demand to do menial jobs that men do," returns Demetrius.

"Like what?" demands Salome.

"Well, when one leaves off doing the important stuff, what is there left to do?"

"Okay, let's not get off course," interrupts Jason. "I think we should stay with what Connor has to tell us about his meeting with Professor McCleaver."

I regather my thoughts. "There were no high places so the people began constructing a tower to make a high place where they could worship false gods. That would have brought humanity back into a mess the likes of which God had destroyed in the Flood. God confused their languages so that they could not communicate with one another. They had to abandon the project."

"There are towers called ziggurats in that area of the Middle East today," offers Demetrius. "It would seem that the people managed to finish their tower regardless of what God did to confuse their language."

"Maybe so," follows Sean. "But it would seem to me that the Babel project would have been delayed until local populations with the same language recovered sufficiently to have enough laborers to do the work."

"That's right," replies Megan. "The Bible says everyone dispersed because their languages were different."

I regain control of the conversation. "Yes. That's what Professor McCleaver said. God delayed the project to give himself time to implement his own plan."

"What plan?" questions Megan.

"He said the act bought God time to implement a new plan to build a holy nation through one man."

"Abraham?"

"Yes. And through Abraham's descendents God would enter the human world as a man."

"That would be Jesus," offers Jason.

"Yes. And McCleaver claimed that through Jesus, God reconciled mankind to himself. That means that the God of the Bible has been, is, and will be interested in and active with the affairs of men. And that means we will always have an absolute."

"Hmmm," mulls Sean. "Maybe that is why McCleaver spent so much time taking Connor through the Bible."

"Could be," replies Demetrius. "According to Connor, McClever has already shown that timelines claimed by other religions are not equivalent."

"Then where does that leave us?" queries Jason.

"I thought we were going to study the Bible," replies Megan.

"Good point," I agree. "Did everyone bring a Bible?"

"I have one," offers Salome.

"Me too," replies Sean.

"Count me in," says Jason as he lifts a Bible from his book bag. Then he turns to Demetrius. "By the way, how far have you read?"

"I got through the Law but I'm now bogged down in the book of Judges."

"Megan?"

"I haven't been doing much lately. I'm still in Genesis. Just starting with Joseph."

"I've got news for you!" I exclaim as faces turn toward me. "The professor is taking over our Bible study."

"What do you mean?" queries Megan.

"I told McCleaver about our starting a Bible study and he thought it is a great thing to do. Then he told me to tell you to skip the Old Testament and read the four Gospels - Matthew, Mark, Luke, and John - this week and discuss them when we meet again next Wednesday. Then I will report back to him next Thursday."

"What do you all think?" queries Megan.

"Wow! Great!" exclaims Demetrius. "That brings a huge amount of brain-power into our study. Lots of stuff we would probably overlook."

"Why not?" adds Jason.

"Okay," Megan replies, "Should all of us read all four gospels or should we break them up in some manner?"

Sean answers. "Why don't we break ourselves into two teams of three and assign Matthew and Mark to one team and Luke and John to the other team. I think it would be wise to spend more time on less than less time on more."

"Fine," I reply. "How about if Jason, Sean, and Demetrius form one team to study Matthew and Mark? Megan, Salome and I will form a second team to study Luke and John. Then we will report back next Wednesday."

"Do you intend for each team to study together?" queries Jason.

"Not necessarily. Do as you wish."

On the following Wednesday the six of us return to Wally's Pub with Bibles in hand. Several bring scribbled notes. We order our drinks and food and, while we wait, Jason begins. "Okay, let's get started. Did everyone finish the assignment?"

He looks around the table as everyone signals in affirmation. Then he continues. "I'm sure you have lots of questions but let's not bog down in details at this time. Let's look at overall impressions. I've classed the books I read into three parts: circumstances surrounding Jesus' birth, his adult life, and his death. So, what are your overall impressions? Let's start with Jesus' birth."

"I now know where Christmas comes from," smiles Megan. "I understand why some churches have those manger scenes."

"Virgin birth??" contributes Demetrius. "I wonder what his DNA looked like."

"Sorry, Demetrius. No detailed questions," scolds Megan. Then she continues in a more pleasant voice. "I was impressed by the angel. I found that God talked with people in Genesis; Noah and Abraham..."

"Add in Moses," interrupts Demetrius.

"...so, I guess God talks with people in the New Testament too."

Sean agrees. "Megan, Jesus is supposed to be God, God come in the flesh. So, yes, God talks with people in the New Testament."

"Perhaps that explains why the two prophets doted on baby Jesus when his parents took him to the temple," I add.

Sean gives me a strange look. "What are you talking about? I found nothing about the baby in the temple."

"That's an account in Luke's gospel. Isn't it in the accounts you read?"

"No."

"Maybe we should shift to Jesus' adult life,"

interrupts Jason.

"Nothing but miracles," replies Sean. "At least that's what I got from reading Mark."

"I found his teachings to be really cryptic," adds Demetrius. "'Blessed are the poor in spirit; for theirs is the kingdom of heaven.' What is that about?"

"Yes, and the parables," complains Jason. "Most of them didn't make sense even after Jesus explained them to his disciples."

I reenter the conversation. "Okay. So Jesus' teachings are cryptic and he heals the sick, raises the dead, and casts out demons. Obviously not an ordinary guy."

"The thing about demons; evil spirits talking through people?" follows Salome. "That makes me feel creepy!"

"Okay, what are your impressions of the circumstances surrounding Jesus' death?" advances Jason.

"He was such a nice guy!" exclaims Salome. "Why would anyone want to kill him?"

"I imagine that going around doing miracles could make someone popular," follows Sean. "At that time

Israel was under the dominion of Rome. Maybe the Romans thought he would get too popular."

"The account I read told that Jesus was convicted of 'blasphemy'," adds Demetrius.

"He swore at somebody?" questions Megan.

"Claiming to be the Son of God."

"What about Jesus' death?" queries Jason, trying to keep the conversation on course.

"Pretty graphic stuff on what they did to him," offers Sean.

"What do you think about the resurrection?"

"Well, he did heal the sick and raise the dead. That is, if the story of Lazarus is true," answers Megan.

Demetrius faces Megan. "It's one thing to raise the dead; it's another thing to raise oneself from the dead. To do that, Jesus would have had to have been the Son of God!"

"Then, do you conclude that Jesus raised himself from the dead?" asks Jason pointedly.

"I don't know. I have no way of knowing whether or not the story is true."

"Sean?"

"There's been a lot claimed about others connected

with gods in ancient history. No claims of anyone raising himself from the dead though. Don't see why Jesus is anybody different. No."

"Connor?"

"If one domino falls, they all fall. At least that's what Professor McCleaver likes to say. If Jesus didn't raise himself from the dead, one domino falls. That means the rest of the story is not true either. The four Gospels claim to be eyewitness accounts of Jesus. It's hard to believe that a story this preposterous could be at the core of a religion that has dominated western culture for the past two-thousand years unless the story is true. But then, all this comes to me as second-hand information. Is the story true or just a truth claim? I don't know. For me the jury is still out."

"Megan?"

"Connor is my teammate," she smiles. "I think I will side with him."

"Salome?"

"No! Jesus spoke in absolutes, some of which I find offensive. Paternalistic! If I accept that Jesus rose, I would have to accept all of his absolutes. That I cannot do. No!"

Jason turns toward me. "Okay, Connor. You still are going to meet with McCleaver tomorrow?"

"Yes."

"Be free to relate our thoughts to him."

"By the way, Jason. What's your verdict on Jesus' resurrection?"

"No."

At two o'clock on Thursday I make my pilgrimage to the faculty lounge. Professor McCleaver is waiting for me.

"Welcome, Connor."

"Professor."

"Did your group complete my Bible study assignment?"

"Yes."

"Any conclusions?"

"We divided up the study into three parts: Jesus' birth, life, and death. Aside from the supernatural stuff, angels showing up at various times, the circumstances surrounding his birth were probably not that unusual for the time. Many of his teachings were cryptic even after he tried to explain them to his disciples. The miracles? Could be true. Then, again, they could be the stuff legends are made of. His death? A lot of people were crucified during that time. He was probably set up by people who didn't like him."

"What about Jesus' resurrection?"

"Of the six of us there were no 'yes's', there were three 'no's', and three demurred for lack of information on the writers and on whether the story is actually true or more like a legend."

"Connor, when we began our sessions, you told me that, of the biblical dominoes, the book of Genesis was the weakest. After we examined the book in more detail you thought the Flood was the weakest domino. That may be true. But the most important domino is not the Flood, but the resurrection of Jesus. Tip this domino and all other dominoes fall with it."

"You mean that, if Jesus' resurrection is not true, then the whole Bible is wrong?"

"Not wrong necessarily, but irrelevant. Tip the Jesus domino and the Bible becomes a compendium of stories and legends that ended approximately two-thousand years ago and has little relevance to us today except perhaps as an historical curiosity."

Professor McCleaver stops for a sip of coffee. Then he continues. "Do you recall what you told me regarding criticisms of the Bible put forth by your religion professors?"

"Yes. Jesus never rose from the dead; miracles never happened; the Bible is full of errors."

"It seems to me that your friends and your professors share similar opinions. Why do you think your teachers were so quick to deny the Resurrection?"

"Well, it was a supernatural event; a colossal supernatural event. I don't think they believe there are such things as supernatural events."

"Yes, but there is more. Think of a high stakes card game. What is the highest card that can be played?"

"The ace of trump."

"In the university system, the full professor is the highest rank among the educators. However, even among these, there are some who stand head and shoulders above the rest in the field of ideas."

Professor McCleaver leans forward in his seat while looking directly at me. "When it comes to teaching, there is one who stands higher than the most distinguished of professors. The resurrection of Jesus Christ is the ace of trump! It is God's stamp of approval on what Jesus taught. Play this card and all teachings regarding life and how to live it, other than Jesus' teachings, are rendered irrelevant! Without question the Resurrection is a 'debate-ender.' It renders Jesus' teachings true. Absolutely! Connor, in order to gain acclaim for their own truth claims, your religion professors have to deny the Resurrection."

Professor McCleaver pauses for another sip of coffee. "Our understanding of the role of the Resurrection is so important that we need to consider your group's conclusions about Jesus' ministry from another perspective. Allow me to explain the Gospel story through an analogy. You may recall that some well-known and highly-respected scientists have proposed that there may exist an infinite number of universes."

I nod. "Yes."

"They put forth that idea in order to save prebiotic evolution. If the probability of prebiotic evolution in this universe is one chance in infinity, then, if an infinite number of universes exist, it just might be that the probability of prebiotic evolution happening somewhere is that one chance. And the universe in which that one chance occurs just might be our universe. Conveniently, we possess no means to discover the existence of other universes so this idea can never be disproven. Nevertheless, some believe it with an incredibly irrational faith."

"I understand."

"Now here's the analogy. Suppose there is another universe out there, a universe so different from ours that we cannot imagine what it would be like. Suppose sentient beings in that universe evolve to where they learn to travel between universes, and suppose one of these beings travels to our universe and finds its way to Earth. Now to keep from freaking us out, the Traveler disguises himself as one of us right down to the DNA. Suppose on some evening our Traveler stands in the midst of a crowd of people and proclaims that he not an earthling but a visitor from another universe. What do you suppose would be the response from those who hear his claims?"

"Laughter, ridicule, derision."

"Yes. And what would the Traveler have to do to prove his case?"

"Prove he is not human."

"How would he do that?"

"Well, he would have to do something we humans can't do."

"What would we call those 'somethings' we humans can't do?"

I am beginning to catch on. I smile as I reply, "miracles."

"Actually, our Traveler faces a host of problems but two stand out clearly to me. First, the Traveler finds that if he is going to convince us of his origin, he will have to do things we humans cannot do, something we call 'miracles.' Second, the Traveler quickly discovers that our language does not contain the words he needs to describe his world..."

I politely interrupt Professor McCleaver, "...so he would make up parables using our language in attempting to communicate what his world is like..."

McCleaver smiles as I continue. "...So that's the riddle of the Gospels. God disguises himself as a man, comes into the world as a baby, grows into adulthood, and then proclaims himself as God. To prove his claim, he does things men can't do – heal the sick, raise the dead, cast out evil spirits – that is, miracles. Then he uses parables because human languages don't have the words he can use to describe his kingdom."

"Yes. Now what would be the greatest miracle our Traveler could perform?"

"I get it! He would have to raise himself from the dead!"

"Correct. And this brings us to the 'last question,' the question I said that, when answered, would drive the final nail into the coffin of postmodernism."

Professor McClever leans back in his seat while looking at me. "Connor, in an earlier session we agreed that an absolute would have to come from a Source or Sources higher than human agency. Do you recall your reply when I asked, 'How could the Source communicate an absolute to humanity'?"

"Perhaps through a prophet?"

"And my reply?"

"Perhaps through a fortune-teller?"

"Connor, you told me that your professors claim that all religions are essentially the same; that the promoters make up rules for the gullible to follow so to avoid the wrath of the 'gods' while claiming that the rules are from the gods. I noted that your religion professors are providing us with an easy path back into postmodernism. What is 'truth' and what is 'truth claim'?"

The professor leans forward while fixing his gaze on me. "How do we know whether the rules are from a non-human agency and therefore can be accepted as absolutes or whether the rules are inventions of human imagination and therefore can be considered as relative?"

"God would have to come in person to tell us like Jesus did?"

"You are close to the answer, but not there yet. Suppose God came in the person of Jesus and gave us absolutes. Once the gospel writers recorded what Jesus said, it became someone else's story didn't it?"

I follow. "And because it became someone else's story, we are back to the 'truth' versus 'truth claim' argument, aren't we?"

"We are. The good news, Connor, is that the Bible answers the question. Today is Thursday. Your group will meet next Wednesday, won't it?"

"Yes."

"Good. I will give you an assignment that you can finish and discuss among yourselves while you are together on Wednesday. Then, on Thursday, come back and we will discuss your answers."

He opens his Bible, extracts a folded sheet of paper, and hands it to me.

CHAPTER 25

# SESSION TWENTY-THREE: FINAL ANSWER

After a meal at the Student Union cafeteria late that evening curiosity overtakes me. I open my Bible and extract the piece of paper the professor had given me. I read his assignment.

*To answer the final question read the following: Chapters 14-16 in John's gospel and Chapters 1-2 in the book of Acts.*

It isn't until Sunday evening that I have time to complete McCleaver's assignment. Because I am on the second team, I am already familiar with John's gospel. However, as I read, I see things differently, because this time I am reading with intent to find references to how God plans to communicate with his followers. I make a list of curious repetitions I had not noticed during my first reading. Then, after reading the first two chapters in the book of Acts, I lean back in my chair, close my eyes, and conclude: *So that is the answer to McCleaver's final question.*

Late Wednesday afternoon I enter Wally's Pub. Demetrius, Sean, and Jason have secured the corner table so our session will again be semi-private. Finally, Megan and Salome arrive. After we place our orders, Jason takes over. "Connor, did Professor McCleaver have any reaction to the conclusions we drew from our Bible study?"

"He sure did! I gave him our verdict on Jesus' resurrection: three of us voted 'no, it didn't happen' and three of us couldn't decide because we have no way of knowing whether or not the story is true."

"How did he reply to that?" queries Sean.

"He claimed that, if Jesus' resurrection is not true, the Bible is irrelevant; it becomes just an historical curiosity."

"Hold on!" exclaims Demetrius. "Is McCleaver telling us that the religion that is at the root of western civilization is just an illusion?"

"That would be the case if Jesus didn't rise from

the dead. So, if McCleaver were here, he would require those who voted 'no' to explain why Christianity has contributed so much to western civilization."

"Well, there were no 'yes' votes so I guess that all you and Professor McCleaver had to work with was our not-so-sure-because-we-don't-know-whether-the-story-is-true votes," follows Megan.

"He considered all of our votes and concluded that we think pretty much like my religion professors do who, he claims, are providing us with an easy path back into postmodernism. What is a 'truth' and what is a 'truth claim'?"

"You mean the question of whether or not the writers of the four gospel books were telling the truth?" suggests Demetrius.

"Yes."

"Lack of credibility is what drove my vote!"

"Mine too."

"Also, mine," adds Megan.

I continue. "That's when Professor McCleaver framed what he calls 'his final question'."

"Which is?" queries Sean.

"How can God communicate with men in ways

that cannot be interpreted as only truth claims?"

Jason leans forward, looking directly at me. "He asked you that question?"

"Yes, one like it."

"What was your answer?"

"God would have to come in person to tell us, like Jesus did."

"And his reply?"

"He said that I am close to the answer but not there yet. Once the gospel writers recorded what Jesus said, it became someone else's story."

"That takes me back to my vote!" exclaims Demetrius.

"McCleaver said that the answer is hidden in some of the books we have read. He gave me a list of chapters in John and Acts as an assignment we can finish here today. Then tomorrow I am to come back and discuss our answers with him."

Jason stops me. "Hold it, Connor. You said McCleaver gave you a list of passages for us to study?"

"Yes."

"Have you had a chance to look at them?"

"Yes."

"Did you find the answer?"

"Yes."

"Then give us the answer," demands Megan.

"I can't. My answer would be just a truth claim. You will have to discover the answer for yourselves. I can guide you along the way if necessary."

"I have the answer!" exclaims Demetrius.

"Then tell us," replies Megan.

"Connor has already given it to us. Once the message Jesus gave was written down, it became someone else's story."

"I don't get it."

"Once the message from Jesus is given, it becomes no one else's story!"

"I still don't get it."

"The message is no one else's story! That means the message comes directly to you!"

"There is no intermediary?"

"No intermediary! God speaks directly to you. That way the message is not a human truth claim; the message is a divine absolute!"

Jason turns toward me.

"Is Demetrius correct, Connor?"

"Yes. Nevertheless, let's go through the Bible passages and see for ourselves what the mechanics look like."

"Everyone, pull out your Bibles," commands Jason.

"Go to the fourteenth chapter of John," I begin. "Since Demetrius has thought out the answer, look for words or phrases that infer how God plans to communicate with his followers."

After a few moments of silence, Salome volunteers, "I have something."

"Go on," I reply.

"The sixteenth verse tells us that God will send another Helper who will be with us forever."

"In verse seventeen it is the 'Spirit of truth,'" adds Megan.

"How about verse twenty-six," follows Sean. "'But the Helper, the Holy Spirit, whom the Father will send in my name, he will teach you all things, and bring to remembrance all that I said to you.'"

"Wow!" exclaims Salome. "Two times in Chapter Fourteen it says the Helper will come to teach us."

"Let's go on to Chapter fifteen," I urge.

"Hmmm," ponders Jason. "It keeps telling us to

abide in Jesus. Do you suppose this is in reference to the Helper?"

"Look at verse twenty-six," exclaims Salome. "More of the same."

"Now let's try Chapter Sixteen," I suggest.

"Wow!" proclaims Megan. "Here is a whole section about the Helper."

"Okay, let's summarize what we have found."

"Easy," proclaims Demetrius. "It's just like I said. God is going to talk directly with his followers. The intermediary is not a human prophet but a spiritual being of some kind."

"I've seen an illustration of a woman with a demon on one shoulder and an angel on the other shoulder, both whispering things to her mind. Do you suppose the 'Helper' is the angel, buzzing around her like a hummingbird?" offers Salome.

"It could be closer than that," I reply. "Look back to Chapter Fourteen at the end of verse seventeen. Jesus says the Helper will be in you."

"Amazing!" exclaims Demetrius. "All this speaks of another dimension, a dimension I've never heard of before."

"Yes, amazing," ponders Jason. "Here we are completing our baccalaureate studies at a major university and we have not been taught one word about this 'other' dimension."

I regain control of the conversation. "Let's bring this study to an end that McCleaver would approve. Let's turn to the first two chapters of Acts. You will find the book just after John."

After a shuffling of pages I continue, "Let's start with Chapter One. Is there anything to add to our understanding of the 'Helper'?"

"Yes, verse five," proclaims Megan. "They will be 'baptized' in the Holy Spirit. Surely that refers to the 'Helper'."

"More than that!" exclaims Demetrius. "Jesus commanded his disciples not to leave Jerusalem until after the 'baptism' had occurred."

"So what?" interrupts Salome.

"The disciples would have to know when the event happened. If they didn't experience the event in some unique, tangible way, they wouldn't have known whether the 'baptism' had happened and when to leave Jerusalem. And look at verse eight! The disciples would receive 'power' when the Holy Spirit came."

"What kind of power?" questions Sean.

"Some kind of power to do things they couldn't do on their own."

"Let's look at Chapter Two," I interrupt.

Demetrius exclaims, "Wow! A violent wind, tongues of fire, speaking in other tongues! That's a memorable experience for sure!"

The group falls silent as we continue reading.

"Okay," I proclaim. "There is a lot more to the story and you can read on. But I think we have the 'last answer' to Professor McCleaver's 'last question.' It's pretty much as Demetrius has said. God is going to communicate to his followers through a spiritual intermediary that he will place within each of them. That puts the issue of 'truth claims' off the table."

The others look at me as I conclude. "I will report our answer to Professor McCleaver when I meet with him tomorrow."

At the appointed time on Thursday, I enter the

faculty lounge and proceed toward the booth where Professor McCleaver sits. As I approach, he lifts his Bible from beside him and places it on the table.

"Welcome, Connor. Did your group complete the assignment?"

"Yes, we did," I proclaim as I sit down across from him.

"Did you find the answer to the 'last question'?"

"I think so. God's plan is to send a Helper, the Holy Spirit, to dwell within each believer. That way God can communicate directly with his followers."

"Correct. The question was, 'How do we know whether the truth claims put forth by religious teachers are really from a non-human agency?' The answer is, 'God would communicate directly to his followers through a spiritual intermediary of his choosing. That means the divine absolutes are within them and there is no need for a postmodern argument regarding 'truth claims.'"

Professor McCleaver smiles as he leans back in his seat. "And so, Connor, central to all of this happening is the ace of trump."

"Jesus' resurrection?"

"Jesus promised to send the Helper to us. He couldn't do that if he were dead! So, not only does the Resurrection validate Jesus' teachings above all others, the Resurrection makes possible the one event – the coming of the Helper – that puts the final nail into the coffin of postmodernism.

"Connor, the resurrection of Jesus Christ is the one domino that men of letters have tried for centuries to tip over. They have failed! The domino still stands!"

Sensing that Professor McCleaver is drawing this session to a close, I reply. "I suppose our having answered the final question brings our sessions to an end."

"It does. However, there remains one issue to be resolved. Turn in your Bible to Acts, Chapter Two."

I open my Bible and locate the passage, "Okay."

"This passage is the account of the coming of the Holy Spirit. Do you believe this story?"

"Er, ah, I suppose so. What do you mean?"

"It is a story written by someone else. Is the story 'true' or just a 'truth claim'?"

"I can't be sure."

"Do you want to be sure?"

"Er, yes, I think so."

"Look closely at the story, beginning at verse thirty-seven. It says, 'Now when they heard this, they were pierced to the heart, and said to Peter and the rest of the apostles, "Brethren, what shall we do?"' Connor, one way the Helper works is by 'quickening' a message in the hearts of listeners so they will know whether a teaching is from men or from God. Look at verse thirty-eight. 'Peter said to them, "Repent, and each of you be baptized in the name of Jesus Christ for the forgiveness of your sins; and you will receive the gift of the Holy Spirit."' This is how new believers in Christ would receive the Intermediary, and from then on, they would be linked to God for direct communication. Now, Connor, look closely at verse thirty-nine. 'For the promise is for you and your children and for all who are far off, as many as the Lord our God will call to himself.' So, Connor, who are those who are 'far off'?"

"I guess that could refer to people living today. We are 'far off'."

"Yes. So how can you know if the story is true?"

"Er, ah, receive the Holy Spirit for myself?"

"Repent, be baptized, and receive the Holy Spirit! At this juncture, our sessions cease being an intellectual discourse and become a personal experience. There is only one way to know whether or not the story is true. You have to experience the Holy Spirit for yourself. Are you inclined to do this?"

I am looking down at the open Bible resting on the table in front of me. My attention is focused on verse thirty-nine and the word 'promise.' Slowly I raise my head to look directly at Professor McCleaver.

"Yes."

CHAPTER 26

# FINAL EXAM

It is the end of the semester. Professor Erik Wadford is giving instructions regarding the final exam set for next week. Then he asks whether there are any questions. A wave of silence sweeps over the room. Sitting in the center section of the lecture hall, about two-thirds of the way back, I raise my hand. Professor Wadford points toward me.

"Yes."

I stand. "Professor Wadford, I have a question about 'relative truth.' Isn't claiming that there are only 'truth claims' the same as claiming that there are no 'absolutes'?"

"Yes."

"And, isn't claiming that there are no 'absolutes' the same as claiming that there is no 'absolute-giver'? And isn't claiming that there is no 'absolute-giver' the same as claiming that there is no God?"

A low murmur rises from among the seated students. Professor Wadford pauses for a moment and then replies. "Clarify for me why you are asking the question."

To be heard over the increasing volume of murmurs, I speak louder. "It seems to me, as you have said, that humans have limited knowledge and so can never know the whole truth about anything, so our claims about truth have to be relative. But a divine being such as the God of the Bible is not limited. Therefore, it seems to me..."

Wadford interrupts, "What you are saying is not news to me. If you take the time to read my credentials you will find that I also have degrees in theology. Whether or not there exists a divine being is not relevant to your question. Whether or not the divine being is omniscient is also not relevant to your question. Once your hypothetical 'god' communicates through imperfect human agents, its hypothetical truth becomes imperfect and therefore relative. Therefore, there can exist no absolutes, God or no God."

Before the professor can end the discourse, I reply loudly. "Then, Professor Wadford, given your knowledge of theology, you must be aware of the 'Helper' that Jesus would send so that God could speak directly to each believer, thereby avoiding imperfect human lines of communication. Consequently, you must be aware that God's messages to his followers can be absolute! Therefore, my question is this: Is your claim that there are no absolutes speculative or definitive?"

Professor Wadford stands motionless beside the podium. As the murmurs increase in volume, I can hear higher-pitched women's voices hurling questions. Then the professor's lips move. Because of the background noise, I cannot hear what he says. But I can see what the professor says. He either speaks the sound or mouths the word.

"McCleaver!"

# QUESTIONS FOR REFLECTION AND DISCUSSION

**Chapter 1**

1. Postmodernism is founded on the premise that there are no absolutes. Do you agree? What are some absolutes you know about? It is argued that postmodernism only questions ideas. Is that true? How can you distinguish between 'false' absolutes (propositions raised up as absolutes but are not) and 'true' absolutes (propositions that are in fact absolutes)?

2. Professor Wadford claims that, through postmodernism, you are free to choose your own values. Why is that not true?

3. Professor McCleaver challenges Professor Wadford's claim that there are no absolutes by asking the question, "Is your claim speculative or definitive?" What do you think he means by "speculative or definitive?"

4. Why do you think Professor McCleaver invaded Professor Wadford's classroom?

**Chapter 2**

1. McCleaver states that 'evolution science' is much like 'forensic science' except that the obvious has been ruled out *a priori*. What does he mean?

**Chapter 3**

1. Connor is given the assignment to find the perfect cereal. He figures he can't for two reasons. First, he has no criteria by which to define a 'perfect' cereal. Second, he doesn't know whether a perfect cereal exists. Are there other reasons for why Connor cannot find the perfect cereal?

2. Connor makes a list of choices for various cereals. Is the cereal most chosen the perfect cereal? Why or why not?

3. Are all truth claims equal? If not, how does one identify the superior truth claims?

4. What does 'cancel culture' have to do with postmodernism? Do you know of someone who was 'canceled'? By whose standards were they 'canceled'?

5. McCleaver claims that he can make his truth claim an absolute. Do you agree? Why or why not?

6. McCleaver argues that there is no way of knowing whether one truth claim is better than any other. Do you agree? Why or why not?

7. Jason makes the statement that postmodernism doesn't lead to personal freedom but leads to tyranny dressed up in a different suit of clothes. Do you agree? Why or why not?

8. Do you know someone who holds to one or more absolutes? Are they considered as intolerant, judgmental, racist, or prejudiced? By whom?

**Chapter 4**
1. Connor states that 'abandoning the absolute does not eliminate the absolute.' Do you agree? Why or why not?

2. McCleaver suggests that postmodernism is a way for elites to create 'false' absolutes. What are some false absolutes currently in vogue in our culture?

**Chapter 5**
1. McCleaver claims that the postmodern promise of autonomy is really a deception because one is not allowed access to all possible truth claims. Therefore one is not autonomous but brainwashed. Do you agree? What are some truth claims you are not encouraged to explore?

2. If there exist absolutes what are possible sources of these absolutes? Who could be absolute-givers?

3. McCleaver offers religion as one source of absolute-giver. What difficulties arise in determining who is an absolute-giver?

4. Why does McCleaver ask Connor if his professors disparaged any religions? What clue does Connor's answers give?

5. What is the foundational narrative behind postmodernism? What would happen if the narrative was overthrown?

**Chapter 6**

1. According to the professor, what is the weakest link in the postmodern narrative? Why is it important to show that this link fails?

2. How did McCleaver show that prebiotic evolution never happened? What was Connor's reaction? Do you find McCleaver's argument convincing?

3. Do you agree with McCleaver's conclusions that, if one domino falls, they all fall?

4. What is Connor's defense against McCleaver's argument? Does it hold up? Why?

5. How has the academic community preserved the postmodernist narrative? Why is it necessary to do so?

6. When Conner returns to his discussion group, what is the group's ultimate conclusion about postmodernism? Do you agree? Why or why not?

**Chapter 7**

1. Connor and the professor begin an analysis of the Bible. What is Connor's approach? Do you agree with Connor? Why or why not?

2. McCleaver tells of a talk by a visiting theologian. What was the theologian's premise? Do you agree with the theologian's premise? Why or why not?

3. Why was McCleaver not convinced by the theologian's argument?

**Chapter 8**

1. At the end of Chapter 6, Professor McCleaver focuses on the authorship of Genesis. Why is knowing who the author is important for accepting the message of Genesis?

2. What is a colophon? What do colophons imply about the literary structure of Genesis?

3. McCleaver offers that Abraham and Joseph assembled Genesis. What is Connor's reaction? Do you agree with Connor? Why or why not?

**Chapter 9**

1. McCleaver and Connor conclude that Abraham was the redactor of the documents produced by his ancestors and his own biography and Joseph was the redactor of the remainder of Genesis. As a third redactor, Moses updated the existing book. This conclusion contradicts the tradition that Moses wrote the book. Do you agree with McCleaver and Connor? Why or why not?

# Chapter 10

1. McCleaver posits that the Flood event was global but the flood waters did not have to cover the whole earth. What mechanisms other than a flood for global destruction can you think of?

2. McCleaver posits that the event causing the Flood was an asteroid impact that broke up the original landmass into continent-sized slabs that rose and fell on waves set up within the mantle. In this case, the depth of the waters was not dependent on the amount of rain. Do you find that McCleaver's descriptions match with the biblical record?

3. McCleaver plots Noah's genealogy from before the Flood with Terah's genealogy from after the Flood. What are the differences between the genealogies? What could have caused these differences?

4. McCleaver postulates two worlds separated by the Flood – the world God created and the rubble of the world God created. In which world do we live? What are some of the differences between these two worlds?

5. McCleaver argues that the Flood is central to understanding biblical history. Tipping this domino tips all the dominoes of biblical history. Do you agree? Why or why not?

6. Connor argues that there exists no geological evidence for a world-wide flood occurring at such a late date as Noah's Flood. Do you agree with Connor?

7. What do you think McCleaver is implying by his statement, "Maybe we don't understand time."?

**Chapter 11**

1. Connor presents his Bible to his study group. In the conversation that follows, Connor states that removing the Bible from schools is the best way of insuring that no one will ever discover an absolute. Do you agree with his conclusion? Why or why not?

2. McCleaver asks 'how do we reconcile Connor's objection to the timing of the Flood with documents written by different authors all of whom claimed to

be eyewitnesses of the events they described?' Is this question an issue for you? How would you answer McCleaver?

3. Connor lists five definitions for time. What is your definition for time?

**Chapter 12**
1. McCleaver shifts from dating Noah's Flood to an analysis of timelines. Why do you think he does this?

2. McCleaver looks at Connor's personal timeline as a tree where the now known past represents the trunk and the future represents the part of the tree with the branches. Why are the branches only on that part of the tree of time that has yet to be lived out? How do you see your personal timeline? Does it differ from McCleaver's definition?

3. The professor labors through the analogy of Jon and Jim during their travel through Flatville. Why do you think he does this? What makes 'equivalence' so important to McCleaver's understanding of time?

4. McCleaver claims that the events experienced by Jon and Jim were equally credible. Do you agree? Why or why not?

**Chapter 13**

1. McCleaver presents a new way for understanding time. Instead of mapping events into timelines, he maps timelines into events. What does this reversal in thinking gain him? How can his new approach to time help him answer Connor's question about the timing of Noah's Flood? Could Jon and Jim's trip through Flatville be similarly mapped?

**Chapter 14**

1. At the beginning of the chapter, McCleaver again stresses that the Jon and Jim timelines are equivalent and the Tom, Dick, and Harry timelines also are equivalent. How does the case of the runners in the foot race differ from the first two cases? Are the timelines in the footrace case also equivalent? How does changing the discussion from different runners to different choices of timelines for a single person change your perception of your own timelines?

2. How does the introduction of the rain shower complicate the situation? Would the fourth runner necessarily have interpreted the wetness on the road to have been caused by rain? What if he/she had seen a fire truck parked nearby?

3. Demetrius concludes that it doesn't matter when a timeline passes through an event but only that it does. Do you agree? What are some implications of this statement?

**Chapter 15**
1. What is Connor's definition for 'halo'? Do you agree with McCleaver's usage of halo for his Event Theory?

2. Do you agree with McCleaver's examples of halo for death, rain at the race, and the resident of Pensacola?

3. How do you react to McCleaver's claim that the 'halo effect' can impact timelines for up to billions of years on timelines that do not intersect with the original event?

4. How does 'heterogeneity of events' in time and space complicate Event Theory?

**Chapter 16**

1. Having described his Event Theory, McCleaver returns to Connor's objection to Noah's Flood. Why do you think the professor began his argument by asking Connor to imagine events for all time within a massive cube?

2. McCleaver simplifies the problem by retaining only those timelines that pass through two specified events and are equivalent. How does that simplify the problem? How many equivalent timelines are left?

3. Connor describes the properties of the two potential timelines that McCleaver selects. Is he consistent with McCleaver's Event Theory? If not, what would you add or subtract?

4. Until McCleaver identified the events 'B' and 'E' as the 'beginning of earth' and the 'ending of earth' Connor was comfortable with Event Theory. What

changed his mind? What does Connor demand? Do you agree with him? Why or why not?

**Chapter 17**

1. McCleaver begins by reviewing the requirements of Event Theory while noting that it remains to prove that the two timelines are actually equivalent. One timeline runs from the beginning of earth to the present in approximately 4.5 billion years. The other timeline runs from the beginning to the present in approximately six thousand years. McCleaver asserts that, in the interim, the two timelines can pass through totally unrelated events. How can the history of earth be explained by two separate and different timelines? Do you think the two timelines are really equivalent?

2. Connor begins by describing a currently held scientific explanation for the origin and history of earth. Do you agree with the five key events of earth history? Why or why not?

3. McCleaver quotes from the Genesis record showing that the Bible records the same five events of creation

in the same order. Do you agree with McCleaver's answer? Why or why not?

4. Do you agree that both timelines pass through the same beginning? Why or why not?

**Chapter 18**

1. At McCleaver's request, Connor gives a summary of five key events that are predicted to occur at the end of earth as we know it. Do you agree with these five events? Why or why not?

2. McCleaver quotes Bible verses that reference the same five key events to occur at the end of earth. Do you think that these verses describe the same end?

3. Do you agree that both timelines pass through the same ending? Why or why not?

4. Are both timelines equivalent?

5. Given equivalence, are both timelines equally valid?

**Chapter 19**

1. How do Connor's friends react when Conner tells them that the two timelines are equivalent? How do you react?

2. McCleaver adds an additional requirement that the equivalent timelines must pass through life-generating events. The current naturalistic geological timeline fails this requirement. Do you agree? Why or why not?

3. Candidates for equivalent timelines passing through life-generating events decline to just two – the modified geological timeline and the biblical timeline. What do each of these timelines reveal about the character of the creator? Which timeline to you prefer? Why?

4. McCleaver argues that timelines for other religious systems satisfy life-generating requirements but are not equivalent. Do you agree? Why or why not?

5. How can the naturalistic geological timeline pass through the haloes of creation events hundreds of millions of years ago when the biblical timeline passes

through the actual creation events a few thousand years ago?

**Chapter 20**

1. McCleaver and Connor begin the session by discussing 'alternate' reality. Do you feel the same as does Connor? Which alternate reality are we in? Are there just two alternate realities or could there be more?

2. Why do you think that the biblical timeline in Chapter 16 was not drawn as the shortest timeline between the beginning and ending events?

3. McCleaver argues that, other than at the beginning and ending events, the two timelines have at least one other event in common, that is the formation of the Jordan Rift Valley (JRV). One timeline has the JRV forming over a period of ten to twenty million years ago. The other timeline has the valley forming over a period of several days. Which answer do you believe is correct? Why?

**Chapter 21**

1. Connor asks his question about the origin of dinosaurs. McCleaver replies that the question takes us into 'alternate realities' regardless of which timeline we use. What are the alternate realities?

2. How does Connor define 'evolution'? How does McCleaver define 'evolution'? What is the difference? Which definition for evolution do you think is more general? Why?

3. According to McCleaver, what are the six mechanisms for evolution? Which are natural? Darwinian? Supernatural?

**Chapter 22**

1. McCleaver claims that some angels rebelled, were cast out of heaven, made their way to earth, and caused chaos within the physical world. What biblical basis is there for such an idea?

2. According to McCleaver the reason for the existence of vicious dinosaurs is genetic manipulation within

existing creatures to produce monsters. Do you think this is a reasonable explanation? Why or why not?

**Chapter 23**

1. Back at his discussion group, Connor tells his friends of McCleaver's answer regarding the origins of nasty dinosaurs. Demetrius takes the information and summarizes his version of the biblical narrative. Do you agree with Demetrius? Why or why not?

2. Jason states why his father in an atheist. Do you think the discussions answer his father's reasons for not believing in God? Why or why not?

3. At his next meeting with the professor, Connor questions the story about the confusion of languages. McCleaver concludes his analysis of the confusion of languages with a statement that the God of the Bible has been, is, and will be interested in and active with the affairs of men and that means we will always have an absolute. Do you agree? Why or why not?

**Chapter 24**

1. Connor and his friends read and discuss the four gospels. Regarding Jesus' resurrection, do you agree with their conclusions? Why or why not?

2. McCleaver claims that Jesus' resurrection is the trump card that cancels all teachings that contradict Jesus' teachings. Do you agree? Why or why not? Why would McCleaver make such a claim?

3. McCleaver tries to explain the gospels by using an analogy of a traveler from another universe. Do you think he succeeds? Why or why not?

4. McCleaver's last question is at the center of postmodernism. Reliability! Are all testimonies reliable? How can we know?

5. How can one distinguish between true and false absolutes?

**Chapter 25**

1. McCleaver gives Connor a short list of Bible passages that he claims hold the answer to the credibility question. Read over the passages. What is the answer to the problem of credibility?

2. After the study group has read through the John passages, Demetrius summarizes the findings. What is his answer? Does it answer McCleaver's final question?

3. Connor concludes that "God is going to communicate to his followers through a spiritual intermediary that he will place within each of them." Do you agree? Why or why not?

4. Communication through a spiritual intermediary puts "truth claims off the table," meaning, postmodernism's claim against absolutes is dead. Why is that so?

5. On their next meeting, McCleaver states the final question and gives the answer. Do you agree with his answer? Why or why not?

6. McCleaver surprises Connor by challenging the credibility of the Acts account of the coming of the Holy Spirit. Is the story true or just a truth claim? How does Connor answer the question? How would you answer the question?

7. How can Connor be sure the story is credible?

8. What is McCleaver's last question? What is Connor's answer? What is your answer?

**Chapter 26**

1. Connor takes Professor Wadford's claims that truth is relative and there are no absolutes to their logical conclusions. No absolutes, no God. Do you agree? Why or why not?

2. Wadford claims there are no absolutes, God or no God. What is the basis of his argument? Do you agree?

3. Does Conner's rebuttal that the 'Helper' makes God's messages to his followers 'absolute' succeed? Why or why not?

4. Connor asks McCleaver's original question. What is his purpose in doing so? How does Professor Wadford react to Connor's question?

# ACKNOWLEDGMENTS

I am grateful to Earl L. Grinols (professor and author) and Anne B. Grinols (professor and author) for their critical reviews of the manuscript and to the editorship of my wife, Sue.

I am also indebted to Mr. Jack McNeil (professional graphic artist) for rendering the manuscript into book format and creating the cover graphics.

# BOOKS BY CLIFTON WELSH
## (AVAILABLE ON AMAZON)

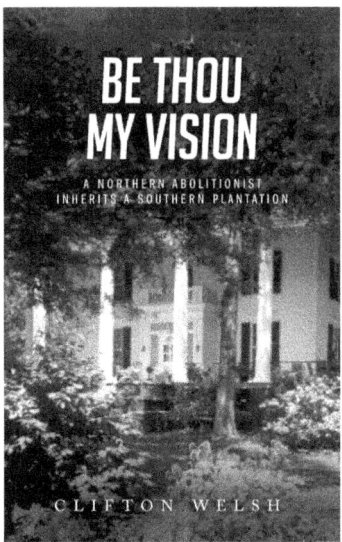

www.ingramcontent.com/pod-product-compliance
Lightning Source LLC
Chambersburg PA
CBHW060820050426
42453CB00008B/520